RIGHT
CAREER
MOVES
HANDBOOK

£6.99
650.14
15975R

RIGHT CAREER MOVES HANDBOOK

Sophie Allen
FOREWORD BY: POLLY TOYNBEE

KOGAN PAGE

Scottish readers should be aware that, in order to simplify the text, the author has referred to NVQs. In nearly every respect, these are the same as their Scottish equivalent, SVQs.

First published in Great Britain in 2003
Reprinted in 2006

Apart from any fair dealing for the purposes of research or private study, or criticism or review, as permitted under the Copyright, Designs and Patents Act 1988, this publication may only be reproduced, stored or transmitted, in any form or by any means, with the prior permission in writing of the publishers, or in the case of reprographic reproduction in accordance with the terms and licences issued by the CLA. Enquiries concerning reproduction outside these terms should be sent to the publishers at the undermentioned address:

Kogan Page Limited
120 Pentonville Road
London N1 9JN
United Kingdom
www.kogan-page.co.uk

© Workthing Limited, 2003

The right of Workthing Limited to be identified as the author of this work has been asserted by them in accordance with the Copyright, Designs and Patents Act 1988.

British Library Cataloguing in Publication Data

A CIP record for this book is available from the British Library.

ISBN 0 7494 4003 1

Typeset by Saxon Graphics Ltd, Derby
Printed and bound in Great Britain by Thanet Press Ltd, Margate

Movers and shakers

Dixons has been shaking things up on the high street for years. But they're not resting on their laurels. The company is as ambitious as ever, continually growing and moving on. And that's what makes it such an exciting place to work, particularly if you're looking for your first job. In fact, Dixons is arguably the most dynamic and fast-moving place to kick off your career.

Moving up

Thanks to some of the best training around, there's lots of scope to develop your skills and move through the ranks – fast. However, as you'd expect from a company of this size, the emphasis is very much on making you feel at home. So, not only will Dixons sponsor and encourage you to gain professional qualifications, they offer excellent facilities too.

All the right moves

In addition to a smart-casual dress code, newcomers will discover warm and welcoming offices, along with a lively social scene and an excellent staff restaurant. Then there's the impressive remuneration package. Dixons offers highly competitive salaries and a range of benefits including a share scheme, a pension (after 2 years), 21 days' holiday (rising after 2 years) and a host of generous discounts.

Get going

There are a variety of openings in a wide range of business areas – IT, Law, Purchasing, Finance, HR, Marketing, Retail, Administration, Buying and Customer Services. But make sure you don't miss out. Find out more about a rewarding career at the heart of Dixons' market-leading business at:

www.careersatdixonsgroup.co.uk

"Studying at Warwick gave me more than an understanding of business. It gave me an understanding of myself."

Yes, you want a globally recognised qualification from one of Europe's top business schools. You want to benefit from high-quality programmes driven by leading-edge international research. But you also want to discover what you are really capable of. Stretch yourself. Build personal skills that will impact on every area of your life. Change the way you think about business - and your own potential.

With internationally renowned degrees from undergraduate to Masters, MBA and PhD, supported by executive development programmes, Warwick Business School is one of the most prestigious business schools in Europe.

To further your career, look no further, call 024 7652 4306 or e-mail enquiries@wbs.ac.uk

www.wbs.ac.uk

  EQUIS ACCREDITED

WARWICK
BUSINESS SCHOOL

Contents

WARWICK
BUSINESS SCHOOL

To further your career... look no further

Whether you have recently graduated and are looking to take further study to start your career on the right foot, or are some years into your working life and want a change of direction, finding the right course is vital.

Warwick Business School, with over 6,000 students on eighteen major programmes, is one of the largest and most established business schools in Europe and one of the largest departments at the University of Warwick.

WBS offers some of the most rigorous, stimulating and highly regarded degrees in business and management, it also holds the highest 5★ rating for international research, much of which feeds directly into teaching. Warwick Business School provides undergraduate, specialist masters, MBA and doctoral research degrees, a growing executive short course, diploma and tailored management development programme, and specialist centres producing leading edge research for policy-makers and leaders in management.

If you choose to study at Warwick Business School you can opt to study full-time, or alternatively, many postgraduate and post experience programmes can be studied part-time to allow you to continue working and apply your learning immediately in the workplace. Either way, you will benefit from the stimulation of a vibrant, high quality student body from a variety of backgrounds.

The University of Warwick is on a spacious and attractive parkland campus and has a full range of excellent accommodation and sports facilities.

Find out more about studying at Warwick Business School.
Tel: 024 7652 4306
or email: enquiries@wbs.ac.uk
www.wbs.ac.uk

THE UNIVERSITY OF
WARWICK

Acknowledgements

Without my experts' help *The Right Career Moves Handbook* would not have been possible, so huge thanks go to Neil Lewis and his staff at Working Careers, Dave Millner, Flemming Madsen, Graham Roadnight, Janet McGlaughlin, Gary Elliot, Jo Buckingham and Dan Crabtree. Thank you also to the interviewees who have provided me (and should provide readers) with great insights into various career paths and hiring manager preferences.

Louisa and Steven, you know who you are and what you did. Thank you for your support.

In 2001-2002, there were 1800 TEFL teachers working in the 129 British Council teaching centres around the world. A staggering 1.1 million class hours were taught around the world by our teachers.

The British Council recruits TEFL teachers and Senior Teachers to work in their centres around the world. All of our schools are in countries where English is not taught as a first language. We require our teachers to have an internationally recognised TEFL certificate (such as the Cambridge CELTA, or the Trinity TESOL or an equivilant), plus two years post qualification experience.

In return, our London contract teachers get a lucrative package, which includes a competitive salary, return flights, baggage allowance and, in some cases, furnished accommodation. The British Council also offers great training and development opportunities to its teachers.
For example, teachers receive funding and support to study for the TEFL Diploma, and there are opportunities to gain promotion as a Senior Teacher, Deputy Teaching Centre Manager, or CELTA tutor. There are also opportunities to get involved in other British Council projects, such as grant-funded projects in education, governance, and training.

The British Council is a great place to work if you are interested in furthering your TEFL career.

For more information, see our website for current vacancies: http://trs.britishcouncil.org

Teach English and
open-mindedness

**At the British Council we look for English language teachers who can
reflect the cultural diversity of modern Britain. We believe in the
principles of equal opportunities.**

As one of the biggest employers of professional English language teachers in the world,
the British Council takes an active interest in the welfare and careers of its teachers.

If you feel that you could rise to the challenge and would like more information,
please e-mail us on teacher.vacancies@britishcouncil.org or telephone 020 7389 4931,
fax 020 7389 4140 or visit our web site.

**BRITISH
COUNCIL**

http://**trs.britishcouncil.org**

Degrees with industrial placements – putting the meat in the sandwich

An industrial placement (or sandwich degree) can have a significant effect on both your degree and your future career. Although not appropriate on all courses, many within the School of Design, Engineering & Computing at Bournemouth University have benefited from this.

So what are the advantages of an industrial placement?

Jo Trenchard, BSc (hons) Business Information Technology – *"During my placement at ICL (UK), I was able to apply the knowledge that I had learnt in the first two years and relate theory to real-life situations."*

Andy Vasey, BEng (hons) Electronic Systems Design – *"My placement year at Sun Microsystems provided me with a comprehensive insight into the electronics industry. I was able to implement methodologies taught to me at University, in areas such as Business, Data Communications, Digital and Analogue Electronics."*

Rob Havill, BSc (hons) Design Engineering – *"My industrial placement provided the impetus for my final year project. Taking a brand new approach to a very real problem has been an exciting challenge."*

What support will you get?

At Bournemouth University, you will get a lot of support and encouragement from the Placement Team to help you find your placement company. Seminars and workshops cover CV writing, covering letters, application forms, interview techniques, advice on how and where to search for company information as well providing placement opportunities. A member of the Placement Visiting Team will also ensure that the work you are undertaken is both relevant and enjoyable.

How do companies view placements?

Karen Bignell of Bignell Shacklady Ewing explains her experience of Beccy Wall – BA (hons) Interior Design student placement from Bournemouth University.

"Beccy has contributed a great deal to the office and got a lot out of her placement for several reasons. She has watched, listened and learnt from the experienced designers and then applied her knowledge gained to the next project. She has taken responsibility for meeting deadlines, and she has asked for opportunities to work on a design or attend a meeting."

Three key questions to ask when considering a masters course

Results found in design, electronics and computing masters courses at Bournemouth University

What are you seeking to achieve?

Many students starting our courses are looking for career advancement/ enrichment. This can be approached in a variety of ways. For example, new EU legislation governing the materials used in both the production and disassembly of products has resulted in a number of students enrolling on the Sustainable Design course. Developing new skills has seen Product Designers joining our Design Psychology course. Embracing new technologies or techniques has resulted in students joining the VLSI & Advanced Digital Design course and the Internet Computing course. For others it has been more fundamental, the need to change direction into something new. This has been true for many on the Computing (Software Engineering) course.

Full-time or part-time?

Many courses can offer full-time or part-time options. So, for example, students might undertake a one year full-time course in Advanced Computing or Interior Design meaning that they concentrate purely on their studies during this period. Others may elect to do the same course on a part-time basis allowing them to continue to work. For some courses such as Advanced Computing this might require studying at the University one afternoon or evening a week, for others such as Interior Design this would mean a study block of one week every term, dependent on the options selected and the period you wish this to be spread across. Typically students undertaking part-time study take two to five years to complete their course.

Who is going to 'teach' you?

Look carefully at the facilities available and the support you will receive and, if possible, look for tutors with knowledge and passion: "Teaching at any level should come from the heart. I have an absolute horror of waking one morning, and finding myself in that academic dead-end where ... 'the notes of the lecturer become the notes of the lectured without passing through the minds of either'. In MA Architectural Materials Conservation, real world practical experience is skillfully interwoven with academic research, and the blend is spiced with passion. I teach it because I want to." – Bruce Induni, Course Tutor

Foreword

With ever-increasing workloads, the challenge for most UK job seekers is in finding the time to manage their careers. This situation is complicated by a growing array of career choices, job hunting techniques and job application processes. Career planning is both a time of excitement and opportunity and a time of anxiety. *The Right Career Moves Handbook* aims, through utilizing a few simple management tools, to reduce the anxiety, help candidates meet their career goals and make successful career moves.

The Right Career Moves Handbook features expert interviews from career management practitioners, senior hiring managers, competency test authors and networking gurus. It is filled with authoritative facts and information and advice for anyone planning their careers. From working abroad to online application etiquette, this careers advice reference tool has answers to a range of candidate queries. Written in a clear, accessible style, it shows how to evaluate oneself, research and weigh up the opportunities, and set goals for the future. It assesses the current job climate, discusses the pros and cons of the various options, and provides strategies to ensure readers get the jobs they want and are best suited to. Regardless of the career stage that a job seeker has reached, *The Handbook* can assist candidates with finding a path to career success.

For careers advisors and career managers alike, *The Right Career Moves Handbook* equips the reader with an insight into current and evolving recruitment practices. This makes it a particularly useful resource for those working with school leavers, graduates and career changers.

Polly Toynbee
Journalist

Wish you could work for an organisation with values that match your own - ambitious, progressive, businesslike? Then wish you were here - at the Environment Agency.

High profile and publicly accountable, we need to take a professional approach to everything we do; whether it's working with government to develop environmental policy, issuing fishing licences or regulating supermarkets!

We have opportunities across a range of specialist areas; soil science, civil engineering, PR, flood protection, HR and IT to name but a few. So, whatever your skills and experience, you could benefit from developing your career with us.

Join us, and you'll find extensive training and development, generous holidays, family friendly provisions well in excess of statutory requirements, final salary pension scheme, flexible working and free personal accident cover.

For information about current vacancies across England and Wales, please visit **www.environment-agency.gov.uk/jobs**

*The Environment Agency is committed
to achieving Equal Opportunities.*

1 Find a job you love

For most of us there is an underlying assumption that as soon as we finish our education we will walk into a job that we love. It is an unsurprising assumption given that we can only specialize in those subjects for which we have shown an expectable level of ability. Some unique individuals decide long before they can speak exactly what they want to be when they grow up, and then go out and do it. The majority, however, feel dissatisfied with their jobs or prove unsuccessful in their job hunt. This can be for a combination of reasons: right job, wrong organization; right organization, wrong job; wrong role; poor remuneration, and so on. Even when people have planned their careers and have found a job they love, they can find themselves mismatched with the working environment. So how can we transform our work and make the right career moves?

First we need to start with us. We have to consider what makes us happy, what we enjoy doing and what we naturally excel at. When we have answered those questions we can start to match desire with destiny. We can begin to identify the jobs that have the best fit with us. *Happy work realities* is the general term that we will use throughout *The Right Career Moves Handbook* to describe: what we know; what we excel at; and what we enjoy doing.

HAPPY WORK REALITIES

- ☐ What I am good at.
- ☐ What I enjoy doing.

There is another component to happy work realities, which is our ideal working environment. This is not merely a case of ergonomics: whether the potted plant on your desk is a yucca or palm. It is more about *living* a happy work reality. An ideal working environment is made up of a complex mix of organizational culture, structure and type. Although these are the main and most influential ingredients, they are not exclusive.

THE IDEAL WORKING ENVIRONMENT MIX

☐ *Work location:* acceptable travel time to and from work.
☐ *Work type:* office based, 9 to 5 or field work, irregular hours, shifts and so on.
☐ *Employment type:* permanent or contract, part time or full time, team work or individual work, job sharing, flexible hours.
☐ *Organization type:* public or private sector, commercial or altruistic, large or small enterprise.
☐ *Organizational culture:* bureaucratic or innovative.
☐ *Organizational structure:* flat, with few department heads, or tall, with many department heads.
☐ *Ergonomics:* open plan corporate office, call centre with booths, home office, factory, retail outlet, restaurant, hotel, gym, submarine, outdoor work, field work and so on.

So finding and attaining a well matched job does not purely decide the right career move. The right job has to be combined with your ideal working environment if you want to live your happy work reality.

The first step of your journey towards your happy work reality is to determine what you are good at and what you enjoy doing. Many of us have obstacles to overcome before we can take the first step.

OBSTACLES TO HAPPY WORK REALITIES

☐ I'm not sure what I'm good at, especially in comparison with others.
☐ I don't like talking about what I'm good at – I'm not a show-off.

For those of you that have difficulty deciding what you are good at, try this approach. Write down how the following people would describe your attributes or achievements:

☐ your boss;
☐ a close friend;
☐ your tutor;
☐ a co-worker;
☐ a relative.

If you have experience of working with more than one of these, include all the relevant descriptions. Once you have written down the descriptions, you will need to decide how well you perform the task. This equates to your level of competence. You could use words to describe your level of competence, but it will be easier to compare your competencies if you rank them. Choose a small range, say 1 to 4, where 4 is high (excellent) and 1 is low (poor). For an example see Table 1.1.

Table 1.1   *Exercise 1: deciding what you are good at*

Description (and person)	Role/responsibility	Competence	Rank
Always hands work in on time (tutor)	Meeting deadlines	Good	3
Keeps cool when the going gets tough (relative)	Stress/crisis management	Excellent	4
Has great ideas (boss)	Innovation/creativity	Good	3
Needs help with report structure/content (co-worker)	Written communication	Average	2

Through completing Exercise 1 you will not only begin to recognize your attributes, but you will be able to describe them, a useful venture in itself. When you come to apply for a job or promotion you will be familiar with indexing what you are good at. However, Exercise 1 is limited on two counts. First, it is a list of perceptions, what you believe your boss, tutor or co-worker would say about you. So because it is subjective it cannot be relied upon in its entirety. Second, as it is based on your experience, it functions in isolation. It does not compare you with other prospective applicants who may compete for the same position. Exercise 1 is a tool that can be used to steer us towards discovering our competencies. To truly understand our attributes we should employ a robust, objective device. For this we need a scientific approach, one that is proven and relied upon by human resources (HR) experts.

Our competencies are determined by two interwoven factors, our abilities and our personality. Abilities and personalities are assessed using tests and questionnaires. The interplay between the two is generally determined by utilizing competency questionnaires. To test our abilities we could use IQ or aptitude tests, and to test our personalities we could use psychometric, motivational or personality questionnaires. The word 'test' is best avoided, as there are no right or wrong answers for questions regarding the characteristics of an individual. By completing personality questionnaires and ability tests we can increase our awareness of what we are good at, what we enjoy doing and our ideal working environment. This will help us to build up a picture of our happy work realities.

Many companies require candidates and existing staff to complete various selection tests. Companies may test the ability, and on occasion compatibility, of their staff for the role that they currently perform. Many companies use tests at the recruitment stage, to support hiring decisions, and they may also use tests as part of selection for promotion. Such tests are either recognized, universal tests (IQ, Myers Briggs Type Indicator) or they are bespoke tests written especially for the company by psychologists.

So sceptics could conclude that even though personality questionnaires are as believable as Agent Mulder's abduction by aliens, they should perhaps practise them anyway as they will undoubtedly have to complete at least one during the course of their career. And spiritualists could conclude that what they learn about themselves through completing these tests will ultimately enrich their lives, their relationships and the universe as a whole!

Mumbo jumbo or not, tests and questionnaires are here to stay. So we thought we'd ask an expert exactly why that is.

Ask an expert

David Millner is a professional competency test author. He writes competency tests (combined personality and ability questionnaires) to meet the recruitment and selection needs of companies. He is the Consultancy Services Director of Psychometric Services Ltd (PSL). PSL assists HR experts and line managers with job analysis, the development of competency profiles, the creation of assessment methodologies and the design of assessment centres. Their task is to understand the hiring and personal development needs of corporates, and deliver practical solutions that yield tangible improvements to them. In the interview below David describes the different types of tests that companies use, and what the results of the tests demonstrate.

What are the different types of test?

Personality questionnaires and motivational questionnaires

The most widely used tests are personality and motivational question-naires. Common ones include the Myers Briggs Type Indicator (MBTI) and 16PF personality questionnaires.

These questionnaires identify the traits of an individual, or an individual's make-up, so they show us *how* an individual *likes to do things.*

Ability and aptitude tests

The second most widely used tests are ability and aptitude tests. These tests are used by prospective or existing employers to establish levels of attainment. They are used to support both hiring and selection decisions.

These tests measure an individual's strengths and weaknesses. They show us what an individual *can do,* and how *easy* or *difficult* an individual finds it to do that.

Can you make sense of words?

Can you make sense of numbers?

IQ tests are a well known example of ability tests; these tests also measure an individual's capacity to reason.

The main difference between personality questionnaires and aptitude tests is that there are *right and wrong* answers for aptitude tests and there are *no* right or wrong answers for personality questionnaires. If in order to get a job or promotion an applicant were to lie when completing a personality questionnaire, he or she should expect to get caught out. This is because personality questionnaires establish how compatible an applicant is with a role. So if an applicant lies, the match is false. The applicant would end up landing in a job or role he or she subsequently didn't enjoy.

For an example of the Myers Briggs Type Indicator personality questionnaire see the boxed example. The traits that are being measured in the example are extroversion and introversion; questions answered with an A indicate extroversion and those answered with a B indicate introversion. For an example of an IQ test see Figure 1.1.

MBTI test paper example

1. Are you

A   easy to get to know?
B   hard to get to know?

15. In talking with friends, do you

A   sometimes tell them a personal thing in confidence, or
B   almost never say anything that you are not willing to have repeated?

Source: MBTI test paper, published by Oxford Psychology Press

---

1. The word 'smart' can be created using five letters from the word 'barnstorm'.

    ○   True   ○   False

2. The digits 08232569 are the same as 96523208 read backwards.

    ○   True   ○   False

3. If a tree branch can hold three people and John weighs twice as much as Adam, and Rachel weighs half as much as Adam, then Rachel, John and Adam can all sit together on the tree branch safely.

    ○   True   ○   False

Source:
http://www.testcafe.com/iqtestiqtest.html

Figure 1.1   *IQ text example*

So where do competency tests fit in? What do they measure?

Competency tests are designed to identify the sorts of behaviours that individuals perceive themselves to demonstrate in the work place. So they measure an individual's attitude about how they perform at work: 'I am good at organizing', 'I thrive on pressure', and 'I would rather work alone'. The questionnaire itself merely asks people about the behaviours that make up a competency, in terms of how proficient the individual perceives him or herself to be. What all of these tests are seeking to identify is the overlap between personal characteristics and attitude (measured by personality and motivational questionnaires), knowledge and experience (tested by ability and aptitude tests) and behaviour (assessed by competency and emotional intelligence tests). The overlap between these areas is what prospective employers want; it's the description of the occupation or job. (For an illustration of this process see Figure 1.2.)

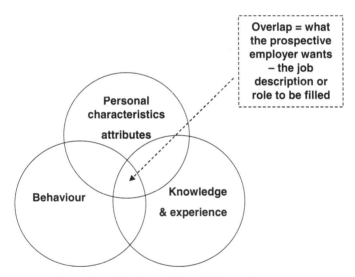

Figure 1.2   _Personality, behaviour and knowledge overlap_

Over the past two to three years there's been a lot of talk about emotional intelligence (EI). What is it?

EI questionnaires try to ascertain behavioural and personal characteristics all at once. They try to identify traits and how you normally achieve tasks. It's not so much what you do, but how you do it, how you accomplish it. As with competency tests the organization is trying to measure individuals' perceptions of how they would behave in certain situations. In particular EI questionnaires try to measure the level of intelligence that an individual has towards emotion. It's certainly important in the working environment that co-workers are sensitive to their colleagues' emotions and reactions to different circumstances. And if your role involves influencing others, then the ability to understand what motivates others becomes increasingly significant. However, personality questionnaires and ability tests already answer the who and what questions, who you are and what you do. They are clearer in their measurement of this because they don't rely as heavily on an applicant's perception of his or her personality and abilities. Characteristics are identified and abilities tested, so the results are a little more objective than the results of EI questionnaires. (See Figure 1.3 for an example of an EI questionnaire.)

1. I get into a mode where I feel strong, capable and competent.

    O Regularly
    O Often
    O Sometimes
    O Rarely
    O Almost never

2. I'm not satisfied with my work unless someone else praises it.

    O Very true
    O Mostly true
    O Somewhat true
    O Mostly not true
    O Not true at all

Source: http://www.queendom.com/cgi-bin/tests

Figure 1.3 *Example of an emotional intelligence questionnaire*

Are there tests that help you to understand the values and culture of an organization?

Some organizations do include questions that are designed to gauge how well an individual will fit to a culture. Psychometric tests measure scale in a fixed way; they measure the accuracy of a fit: from point A to point B and how near or far an individual is to a point. Scale can be measured in a fixed way because every answer counts towards a trait identifier. For example in the Myers Briggs Type Indicator the characteristics of extrovert and introvert are measured, so that an individual will either be defined as an extrovert or an introvert. The meanings of organizational descriptions, however, vary from organization to organization. For these reasons they cannot be as accurately measured as psychometric questionnaires. What counts as a 'go-getter' attitude for a charity fundraiser may vary enormously from a 'go-getter' attitude for an investment banker. It's best to talk to someone who works for the organization in a similar role to the one that you hope to fulfil. However, if you do find yourself taking a personality questionnaire, try to remember as much about the test as you can. It will describe the job and area or department that you want to operate in, and amounts to a very detailed job description.

Are there tests that can match me to working environments?

There are some on the market, though their usage is limited. It's far better from an applicant's perspective to use realistic job previews such as video footage of a company, a line manager, or employee currently employed in the role that you are applying for. If you're going to work in a call centre, walk around and see if you would like working in a booth. Meet and greet employees in the company and get to know them. An interview with your prospective employer can cover most of these points, whether the interview is a telephone or a face to face one.

What is the purpose of these tests?

To provide an employer with an indication of an individual's ability to do what he or she is being tested on. From the results of these tests an employer will get an idea of how suitable or able a candidate is. As a candidate it's important to remember that there is no such thing as a perfect test. Human judgement does play a part. Most job offers are actually decided at the interview stage. The results of the company's test, combined with an interview, help to build a picture of a candidate. A hiring decision shouldn't be based on the results of the test alone, because both the interview and the test results are just snapshots. Combining the two optimizes a much more powerful hiring decision.

The Rapid Personality Questionnaire

The Rapid Personality Questionnaire (RPQ) is a validated psychometric measure that has been created by PSL to assist with the selection and development of personnel. The RPQ contrasts a person's responses with those given by a general sample of the working population. The standardized factor scores range between 1 and 19, with the average score band of between 9 and 11. The text report should be read in this context, with due regard given to the requirements of a person's current or proposed role. As with all psychometric measures, the RPQ scores should be used in conjunction with other sources of information on the individual, such as an interview and CV, and should not be interpreted in isolation.

How are the tests scored?

Ability tests are scored like maths tests, with a mark out of a total. In the case of IQ tests, the marks are banded. A mark in the range of 144 to 160 inclusive would identify a high IQ individual, termed 'gifted'. Personality questionnaires measure on a fixed scale how well the individual fits the trait that is being analysed. Results are presented as bar charts or in some cases a curved line on a graph. All of the HR experts that PSL works with are trained in test results analysis. When a test is first written, a profile of the ideal candidate is produced. The profile can be presented as a graph, score sheet or bar chart. Its purpose is to facilitate gap analysis between the ideal profile and the candidates' test results profiles. Many organizations use the analysis of test results as a basis for interview. The interviewer can discuss any differences between an applicant's profile and the ideal profile during the interview.

IDENTIFY HAPPY WORK REALITIES

To recap, your happy work realities are:

- [ ] what you're good at;
- [ ] what you enjoy doing;
- [ ] your ideal working environment.

To make the right career move you need to understand these fundamental elements of what makes you happy. You can discover your happy work realities in a number of different ways. To assess what you are good at, you can either self-assess or scientifically test your abilities.

HOMEWORK TIME: EXERCISE 2, ABILITIES ASSESSMENT

If you already know what you are good at, scoring your level of ability is relatively straightforward. Abilities can be ranked simply using a small range of 1 to 4, where 1 is low (poor) and 4 is high (excellent). Starting with what you are best at, begin to rank your abilities. For the rest of this chapter we'll use an imaginary job candidate as an example: see Table 1.2 for her self-assessment.

Table 1.2   *Exercise 2: ability example*

Ability	Rank (where 1 is low and 4 is high)
Numeric	4
Pattern recognition	3
Communication, verbal	3
Communication, written	2
Creative	1
Spatial orientation	1

If you prefer a scientific approach there are various sources of professionally authored tests. Several Web sites offer free IQ tests: the tests are timed and take from 12 to 20 minutes. Or you could arrange for a local Mensa test administrator to visit your home and administer an IQ test (tests can be booked online via http://mensa.org.uk). Of

Academic qualifications might not always help to ensure that you have the skills you need for the job you want. Vocational qualifications do – it's why they exist. And if you want your certificate to be awarded by a name that will impress employers, City & Guilds is the one to choose.

City & Guilds is a household name – in fact, according to recent Consumer Surveys, one in five households has a City & Guilds qualification. City & Guilds is the leading vocational awarding body in the UK, awarding almost 50 per cent of all National Vocational Qualifications (NVQs). We're global too, providing internationally recognised qualifications across the world. As the only awarding body solely dedicated to vocational learning, we offer companies worldwide a recognised skills benchmark.

There are more than 6,500 approved City & Guilds centres in the UK, offering more than 500 qualifications in almost all career sectors – from agriculture to hairdressing, from health care to IT, and from teaching to vehicle maintenance. We provide a wide range of office-based qualifications through City & Guilds Pitman Qualifications, and a comprehensive set of management awards through the Institute of Leadership & Management (ILM).

Our qualifications are available at all levels, from entry to the highest levels of professional ability. You can choose the level that's right for you and progress as far as you want, at a pace that suits you. So, whether you are just starting your career or moving up the job ladder, City & Guilds should have exactly the qualification you need.

Check out our website, **www.city-and-guilds.co.uk**, for more details, and to access a qualification finder that will locate the nearest centre that runs the course you are interested in. Or get more information from our Customer Relations Team, by phoning **020 7294 2800**, or e-mailing **enquiry@city-and-guilds.co.uk**

City& Guilds

Don't forget vocational qualifications!

City & Guilds offers over 500 vocational qualifications providing skills for a brighter future, skills which could help you find a responsible, rewarding and fulfilling job. Research indicates a national skills shortage in the coming decade, so build a real future for yourself with a City & Guilds qualification. Check out our website – you'll be surprised at the range of qualifications!

course IQ tests are also available offline. For further information about sources of tests see Appendix 1.

What we are good at is influenced not just by our level of intelligence (IQ or aptitude) but also by our personal characteristics, in particular our attitude towards the task in hand. Are we motivated or demotivated by a challenge? Do we perform better in pressurized situations, or do unplanned events throw us off course? It is equally important therefore, when assessing what we are good at, that we understand not just whether we enjoy it, but why. This can be realized through understanding how personal characteristics lead to success.

PERSONALITY ASSESSMENT

Personal characteristics, unlike abilities, are measured, not tested. Characteristics are measured on a fixed scale, so it can be shown how well the individual fares in the trait being analysed. Though individuals can gauge their own personal characteristics, attitude and motivation, they cannot measure them or define them scientifically. For this we need to use recognized psychometric questionnaires and their resultant informed terminology. Much like David Millner's example of the differences in meaning of a 'go-getter' attitude from one organization to another, our understanding of 'go-getter' is subject to our own prejudices of interpretation. If we are to succeed in our career moves we need to understand the language of personality questionnaires. We need to be able to rely upon an objective understanding of our personal characteristics, because this affects our performance at work. Through understanding our work preferences we will increase our ability to identify jobs that truly match our personality and abilities.

You can scientifically access, for free, personality, EI and competency questionnaires online via the sites mentioned in Appendix 1. These sites are a good place to start to identify your happy work realities, and practise your questionnaire and test techniques. If you would rather complete your questionnaires offline, see the books listed in Appendix 1. Most of them feature tips on how to improve your performance.

Once you are familiar with your abilities and personality, you will understand your competencies. Competencies, as we know, are the nucleus of a job description; they are what the prospective employer wants. Your competencies are the core of your profile: what you are good at, what you enjoy doing and your ideal working environment.

If you are already aware of your competencies, try Exercise 3 instead of Exercise 2. Starting with the responsibilities of the job that you are currently doing, or last did, describe your competencies and score them. If you are not currently working, analyse an interest that you have (see Table 1.3 for our imaginary candidate's examples). This exercise is easy to complete if you understand your level of attainment in comparison to others. If you struggle to fill in the gaps, try completing an ability test, personality or competency questionnaire first.

Table 1.3   *Exercise 3: competency example*

Job/interest	Role/responsibility	Competency	Score
Customer care	Update customer records	Accurate/fast data entry	4
Customer care	Update customer records	CRM* IT skills	4
DIY	Redecorate spare room	Set and manage budget	3
Learning French	Complete course	Speak French – fluent	4

* CRM: customer relationship management

Once you have assessed your levels of ability, repeat the process, but this time grade the ability or competency by how much you enjoy the activity, as in Exercise 4 (see Table 1.4). By highlighting how much you enjoy the activity, you can begin to uncover what motivates you. Your attitude towards your work has a profound effect on how successful you are at it. As before, score 4 as high and 1 as low.

Table 1.4   *Exercise 4: enjoyment grade competencies example*

Job/interest	Role/ responsibility	Competency	Enjoyment grade + description
DIY	Redecorate spare room	Set and manage budget	4 Interesting to work out budget and motivated by cost savings/ bargains
Learning French	Complete course	Speak French – fluent	4 Enjoy verbal exercises
Comic impressionist	Perform as stand-up comic – make the audience laugh	Communication, verbal	4 Get a kick out of performing as comic impressionist
Customer care	Update customer records	CRM IT skills	3 Like to improve IT skills
Customer care	Update customer records	Accurate/fast data entry	2 A bit boring

Exercise 5 builds on the previous exercises to identify work preferences. Do you work better alone or as part of a team? Completing this exercise will provide you with an accurate indication of the type of organizational structure that you prefer. It is the skeleton for your ideal working environment, because it deals with your immediate environment. Your 'near environment' is the one you have the most influence over.

Think about your current working environment or how you like to complete tasks. Describe how you accomplished an activity, and score the accomplishment for satisfaction. So if you were pleased with the way you accomplished a task, give it 4 out of 4. You can use the same tables as before, but replace ability with the way in which you fulfil the role, responsibility or interest. Our imaginary candidate's assessment is in Table 1.5. You should also consider the ergonomics of your environment: whether you prefer to work in an office, from home or outside.

Table 1.5   _Exercise 5: work preferences_

Job/interest	Role/ responsibility	How	Work preference
DIY	Redecorate spare room	Collaborated with partner re budget	4 Prefer to have the reassurance of a second opinion
Learning French	Complete course	Classroom based part time course + mentor + distance study	4 Like being able to call mentor
Customer care	Update customer records	Work alone/ devised own error-checking system	2 Wasn't sure I got it right
Customer care	Update customer records	Updates delivered as online learning via the intranet	1 Found it tough to get started

Once you have completed your self-assessment you can start to piece together your profile. For a tabulated version of the example profile see Table 1.6, and for a drawing of it see Figure 1.4.

Table 1.6 *Happy work realities example*

Job/interest	Role/responsibility	Ability/competency rank	Enjoyment grade	Work preference
Brain teasers	N/A	4 Numeric	4 Good fun	N/A
Customer care	Update customer records	4 CRM IT skills	4 Enjoy improving skills	1 Found it tough to get started
Comic impressionist	Perform as stand-up	3 Communi-cation, verbal	4 Get a kick out of performing	4 Like to check material with friends
Customer care	Update customer records	4 Accurate fast data entry	2 A bit boring	2 Wasn't sure I got error checking right
DIY	Redecorate spare room	3 Set and manage budget	4 Interesting to work out budget and make savings	4 Prefer to have reassurance of second opinion
Learning French	Complete course	4 Speak French – fluent	4 Enjoy verbal exercises	4 Like being able to call mentor

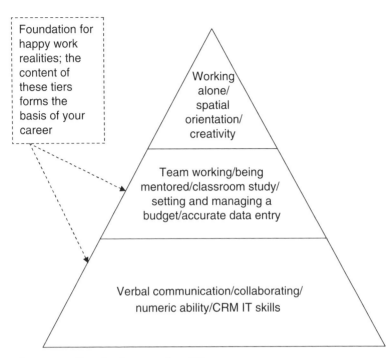

Figure 1.4 *Drawing happy work realities*

ASSESSMENT CONCLUSIONS

In these examples our sample candidate enjoys verbal communication and being creative, even though these are not abilities she excels at (see Tables 1.2, 1.3 and 1.4). She does not enjoy using one of her greatest skills, accurate data entry, as much as setting and managing a budget, a function she does not currently perform at work. As you can see from Table 1.5 (work preferences), even when working in an area of high competence (numeric ability) she is unsure of her level of attainment when she works alone. It follows that this candidate would not thrive in a home working environment, and that she is better suited to working as part of a team or with the support of a mentor.

It seems that this person would enjoy applying numeric theory in her work, perhaps by setting budgets to help reduce costs for her company. She might develop her career by, for example, asking to embark on team customer relationship management (CRM) training at work, or volunteering to assist the accounts department in a project to reduce customer service call charge costs. If she manages this, she will have changed her role and increased its match to her happy work reality.

MATCH HAPPY WORK REALITIES TO ROLES

Once you have completed your profile you can start to match yourself to suitable roles. Descriptions of roles can be found in various places. The Careers and Occupations Information Centre (COIC) publishes an annual book, *Occupations*, which contains information on hundreds of roles and careers; it can be found in library reference sections. The descriptions are quite in-depth, and cover the type of work and working environment associated with the occupation. The online equivalent of this may be found at: www.prospects.ac.uk. For an example of a sales manager occupational description see the boxed example.

Example: sales manager occupational description

The work
As a sales manager, it's your job to organize your team of sales reps and help them do their job of selling products and services.

Sales managers – sometimes called area or regional sales managers – work closely with both their marketing department and the sales reps in the field, translating the marketing plan into sales targets for the team and individual sales people.

It's a job that needs a wide range of skills. You'll usually recruit and train your sales force, and introduce new and existing staff to new products or sales schemes at sales conferences. You'll organize the sales force, allocate areas,

---

and compile and analyse sales using a computer. You have to keep a close watch on performance, which could mean operating incentive schemes or finding other ways to motivate staff to reach their targets.

Some sales managers deal with a few major customers themselves, and you might be called in to sort out more serious problems or complaints. A very important part of your job is sending customer and market research information back to head office. What you learn in the field can have an impact on product development, manufacture or promotional strategies.

Skills and interests
To be a sales manager you need:

- ☐ a wide range of personal and business skills;
- ☐ to be good at working with people, in groups and one to one;
- ☐ strong motivational skills and good management ability;
- ☐ initiative and enthusiasm;
- ☐ an excellent knowledge of your products and those of competitors;
- ☐ good communication skills;
- ☐ good organizational and admin skills, especially in working with figures;
- ☐ the ability to work calmly under pressure;
- ☐ skills in IT and, for overseas work, in languages – they are becoming more important;
- ☐ a driving licence – this is essential.

(Source: provided courtesy of Working Careers)

Another source of information about occupations is the job descriptions in job advertisements: online, in newspapers and in the trade press. When you read ads for vacancies, make a practice of highlighting the minimum skills, qualifications or years of experience that are required. This will help you to become familiar with what prospective employers are seeking. In addition you can start to match your happy work realities to job descriptions.

You are now on track to realize your career ambitions, so the next step is to plan for success. The following chapter focuses on the 'reality' part of happy work, and in so doing builds the foundation for future right career moves.

2 Plan for success

The most fateful component of a right career move is self-belief. Attitude will either limit or expedite success. But even if you began with more confidence than a pop diva, a little rejection and the occasional disappointment can corrode away resolve. One way to combat this and ensure consistently high levels of self-esteem is by having a career plan to fall back on. Just as top athletes and performing artists rely on their training to overcome obstacles, a plan can be treated as a career moves crutch to be leant upon during difficult times. A plotted career path provides a bedrock to bolster motivation during periods of uncertainty. Designing a robust plan is reliant upon identifying appropriate career path options. Through creating and finding options the road to career success is rooted in fact not fiction. In this way career move success is founded in a strategy that fosters positive attitudes and high levels of self-belief.

DRAW WHERE YOU ARE

The starting point of your career path, and therefore the plan, is when you leave school, college or university. As people progress through their career they take different routes depending on their circumstances at the time. So in order to understand how you have arrived at your current job, you need to locate it in your career path. This is achieved by going back through your work history to higher education, and drawing what you have done up until the present time. See Exercise 1, as exampled in Figures 2.1 and 2.2.

Exercise 1: drawing a career path

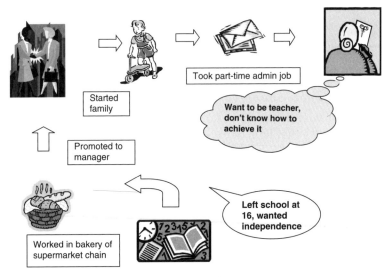

Figure 2.1 *Drawing of a parent's career path*

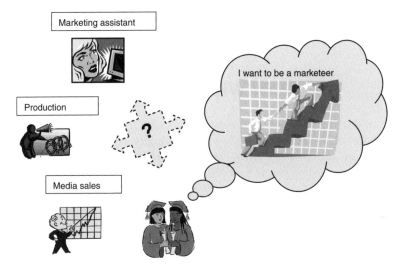

Figure 2.2 *Drawing of a student's career path*

We are not looking for the next Turner Prize winner here, but rather a way of putting down on paper where you are in your career path. If you would rather write than draw, you can represent your career path as a CV-type work history. By examining our past careers we can interpret the moves that we have made. You should look out for any patterns that you see emerging:

- ☐ Have you jumped from one job to another?
- ☐ Have you approached different career moves in a structured way?
- ☐ Have you taken a steeper route to save time, or worked harder for less money in order to gain experience?

By recognizing why you made your past career moves, you can use your past to forecast future career dynamics. You should now appreciate how you are likely to behave when faced with future career choices. Your work history will also indicate what circumstances have led to better or worse career moves. It is valuable to recall what was good about your previous roles, and not just what was bad. Through this you can determine how well your previous roles matched your happy work realities, so in the future you should be able to avoid the worst and embrace the best.

FACE CONSTRAINTS

Now that you understand your career history, you can learn from your past experiences and manage your next career move smoothly. We manage our career moves more effectively when we work with, not against, the demands and constraints of our lives. Maybe you have dependants whose care needs limit the number of hours you can work. You might need specialist qualifications, or to gain another year's experience in a particular discipline. You might be relied upon to contribute financially to the upkeep of your household, so you cannot realistically do without an income for any length of time. All these constraints, usually associated with either time or income, must be taken into account in your career plan.

SET A COURSE

Before you can draw up a career plan you need to decide on the best route to take you to your next career move. This is like a mini career path, which starts with where you are now and ends with your happy work reality. From the range of routes that you draw, one path will satisfy your demands, constraints and choices best, and that will lead to your occupation or roles matches. So taking the parent candidate from Figure 2.1 as our example, we can survey the different routes that are available to her.

Routes to teaching

If our candidate wants to be a teacher, she will need to obtain a degree and complete a postgraduate certificate of education (PGCE), or complete an Initial Teacher Training (ITT) course. She will hopefully be able to find a university or ITT course provider that does not require her to complete A levels first, if she makes a case for her previous work experience and company training to be accepted as an alternative. In this case, she worked in a management role for several years, and if she completed work-related training during this time – for example, on stock inventory control, budget management, IT office skills or people development skills – she could ask for that to be taken into account.

If you find yourself in a similar position, try to make full use of not just your experience, but also any industry-specific courses that you have completed. Many Modern Apprenticeships, National Vocational Qualifications, City and Guilds and certificated IT qualifications can be treated as contributing towards a degree, or other further education courses. For our sample individual's range of routes to her happy work reality, see Figure 2.3.

In our example the candidate has four options to choose from: two opportunity routes, as shown in Figure 2.3, and two alternatives for each, studying full time or studying part time. Opportunity 1 is quicker but more expensive, especially if the full time study route is chosen. Opportunity 2 is slower and more affordable, but will not qualify her to teach at a state school, which could mean she will find it harder to get a good job. She is

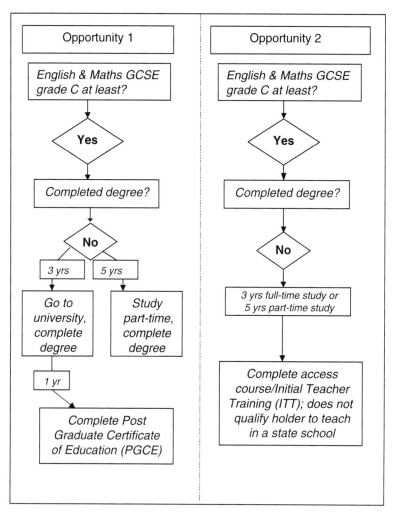

Figure 2.3 *Qualifying to teach*

likely to find arguments for and against each option, and to be sure she makes the right choice she will need to appraise each option systematically.

EVALUATE OPTIONS

Most of us will have more than one route to our next career move. Picking the right route can be confusing, and the choice has an obvious bearing on the outcome. Before deciding on what path to take, you should evaluate your options. You may want to do this with family and friends, as the route that you choose will affect the lives of those closest to you.

There are two standard ways in which you can evaluate options. You could weigh up the pros and cons of an option (see Table 2.1) or you could use the more sophisticated SWOT analysis (see Tables 2.2 and 2.3). SWOT analysis is where a choice is categorized in terms of: strengths, weaknesses, opportunities and threats prior to making a decision. SWOT analysis is a useful evaluation tool when trying to understand what impact choices made *now* might have in the *future*.

Table 2.1   *Pros and cons career path analysis (parent example)*

Pros	Cons
Opportunity 1, full time	**Opportunity 1, full time**
Quick – 4 years in total	Costly – will not be able to work
Will be qualified to teach in state	May incur debts through studying
school – greater job opportunities	Will not have enough time for
Term holidays will coincide with	dependants during term times
dependants – reduced cost of	May not be able to do school run
child care	
Opportunity 1, part time	**Opportunity 1, part time**
Cost effective, should be able to	Longest option to complete,
continue to work part time	6.5 years rather than 3 years
Should still have time for dependants	Term holidays may not coincide
Will be qualified to teach in state	with dependants – may still have
school – greater job opportunities	to pay for child care
Should be able to do school run	
Opportunity 2, full time	**Opportunity 2, full time**
Quickest option – 3 years in total	Costly – will not be able to work
Combines studying for a degree with	Will incur more debts
teaching skills – learn from one	Will not have enough time for
institution – continual assessment	dependants during term times

Term holidays will coincide with
dependants – reduced cost of child care
Private/one to one teaching increases
work hours flexibility – reduces child
care constraints/demands

Will not be able to teach in state
schools – fewer job opportunities
May not be able to do school run

Opportunity 2, part time
Cost effective, should be able to
continue to work part time
Combines studying for a degree
with teaching skills – learn from
one institution – continual
assessment
Should still have time for dependants
Private/one to one teaching increases
work hours flexibility – reduces child
care constraints/demands
Should be able to do school run

Opportunity 2, part time
Long option to complete – 5 years
Term holidays may not coincide
with dependants – may still have
to pay for child care
Will not be able to teach in state
schools – fewer job opportunities

Table 2.2   _SWOT career path analysis (parent example) for_
opportunity 1, part time

Strengths
Cost effective – should be able to
continue to work part time
Should be able to spend time with
dependants

Weaknesses
Slowest option – 6.5 years
Term times may not coincide –
child care costs possible

Opportunities
Will be qualified to teach in state
school – increased job opportunities
Will be able to focus on degree
Will be able to focus on certificate of
education (PGCE)
Should be able to work around
collecting kids from school

Threats
Work hours are set
Pay scales are set
May have to change institutions
– mentors – may not do well
Difficult to juggle demands
Long time to stay focused/
motivated

Table 2.3   *SWOT career path analysis (parent example) for opportunity 2, full time*

Strengths	**Weaknesses**
Quickest option – 3 years	Costly
Learn from one institution, combine degree and teaching skills	Not qualified to teach in state schools so reduced job opportunities
Opportunities	**Threats**
Start to earn money sooner	Will incur more debt than if a slower route was taken
Term times coincide with children – could reduce cost of child care	May have to study during term times
Better quality time with children	May find the pace too fast – get left behind
Should have same mentor(s) to help	May have to take work as and when it comes up; may conflict with quality time with children and child care
More flexible work hours	Will struggle with school run

If you choose to apply a SWOT analysis to your career path options, you will find that the strengths and weaknesses impact your *current* situation, and opportunities and threats influence your *future* situation. When analysing options, consider whether your current constraints and demands will be the same in the future. For example, the age of your children might affect the option you choose. If three years hence your children will not need to be collected from school, you only need to consider that constraint for three years. This is the case for our sample parent, so in Table 2.3 the school run appears in the threats column, because the total duration of opportunity 2 (full time) is three years.

In the example the person's primary constraint is financial. The most affordable training course, with the best remuneration at the end of it, is opportunity 2 (part time), and she will probably choose that option.

PLOT A COURSE

Once you have decided on the best route to your happy work realities, the next phase is to plot your career path. Your career path will be delineated by what you must achieve in order to reach your destination job. Having identified your target achievements you should set objectives to ensure that you complete them, and progress towards your destination job. Objective setting, therefore, forms the basis of your career path and your career plan. If you use a simple format to define your objectives you should be able to monitor your advancement effortlessly. A popular objective setting method is to ensure that they fit to SMART criteria. Your objectives should be:

- ☐ **s**pecific;
- ☐ **m**easurable;
- ☐ **a**chievable;
- ☐ **r**elevant;
- ☐ **t**imely.

An example of a non-SMART objective is the statement 'I will win *Big Brother*'. This objective is neither relevant nor timely. It may be achievable, and it is measurable. A SMART version of this objective could be, 'I want to win the next *Big Brother*, because if I do, I will be famous and I could be offered a job as a TV presenter.' This objective is specific, measurable and, judging by those that have won it before, completely achievable. It is relevant to a SMART objective setter because it should further an entertainment career, and it is timely as the person aims to win the 'next' *Big Brother*.

Set SMART objectives

Taking opportunity 2 (part time), our example parent might map the following SMART objectives (see Table 2.4):

- ☐ Attend next local college open evening to enrol on next ITT course.
- ☐ Become member of local parents' association.
- ☐ Organize school run sharing roster with friends/neighbours.
- ☐ Speak to bank about loan.

☐ Collate training/further education certification for ITT enrolment form.
☐ Prepare study plan with family.

Table 2.4   *SMART objectives time-map for option 2, part-time*

Time	Objective
November	Speak to bank about loan Organize school run sharing roster with friends/neighbours
December	Become member of local parents' association Collate training/further education certification for ITT enrolment form
January	Attend local college open evening to enrol on ITT course
February	Prepare study plan with family

The SMART objectives detailed in Table 2.4 are short term. It is possible to draw up long-term objectives based on options analysis and objective setting, as described above. Once these objectives have been established you could formulate a long-term action plan (see Figure 2.4 for long-term career plan examples). You should include milestones in your career plan to mark achievements. It is easy to lose sight of objectives if achievements are not recognized and rewarded. Job seeking is hard work, often time-consuming and sometimes clandestine. By honouring your successes you should continue to complete short-term objectives and in so doing travel towards your destination job.

You will notice that our example parent aims to network and gain teaching experience in the penultimate year of her five year plan, even though she plans to enter a profession where jobs tend to be comparatively easy to obtain, and where the barriers to entry and demands for previous experience that are associated with career changes are comparatively low. This is because she knows that when she starts job seeking she will be competing with experienced hires and young graduates who have several more years of future service to offer, and she will need contacts and experience in order to improve her relative chances. To expedite a successful job

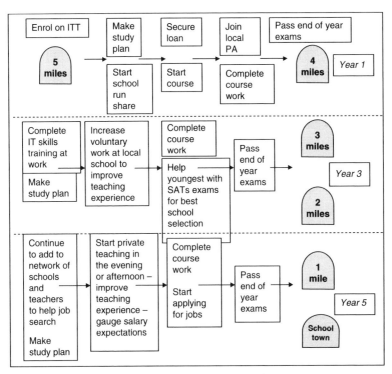

Figure 2.4 *One, three and five year career plan*

search it is useful to recognize the type of job seeker that you are. By knowing your job seeker type you can turn threats to opportunities. As in the example you can tackle any weaknesses that you may have, and maximize your potential.

JOB SEEKER TYPES

A career path can be split into several different stages that are described by job seeker type. The main types of job seeker are listed in Table 2.5. In Figures 2.5 and 2.6, the two sample individuals we have discussed, the parent from this chapter and the student from Chapter 1, apply job seeker descriptors to their different career moves.

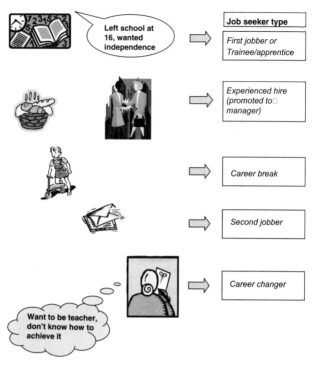

Figure 2.5 *Parent's career path by job seeker type*

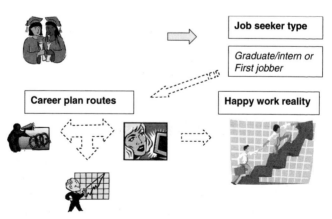

Figure 2.6 *Student's career path by job seeker type*

Table 2.5   *Job seeker type guide*

Criteria	Job seeker type	Job type
Left school (did not take further education)	First jobber	Trainee or junior position
Started course (eg NVQ/ City and Guilds) soon after finishing school/college	Trainee/ apprenticeship First jobber	Trainee or junior position
Started degree soon after finishing school/college	Graduate intern Graduate trainee First jobber	Internship Graduate fast track Junior position
1.5–5 years' experience in current role with existing employer	Experienced hire	Promotion or specialization with existing employer
1.5–5 years' chronological experience within same sector or same occupational group	Second jobber	Promotion or specialization within same sector or same occupational group
Less than 1.5 years' experience in sector or occupational group	Career changer	New job within different sector or different occupational group

Our parent has been a first jobber/trainee, an experienced hire, a second jobber, and is now embarking on a career change. In contrast to the student, she cannot commence her new career as a graduate intern, because she will have studied as a mature student.

A shortage of teachers has created a high demand for them, and led to government support for recruitment initiatives. This has resulted in the introduction of fast-track schemes, the purpose of which is to attract career changers. In addition the entry level requirements have been reduced, previous experience is not necessary, and rules about the degree subject chosen and level of attainment achieved have been relaxed. Most new careers are harder to break into. Many career changers face a drop in income, and possibly a slow ascent from a junior position. This is frequently because hirers look for previous experience.

Though previous experience cannot be replaced by qualifications or transferable skills, knowledge, a powerful network and relevant skills can be traded against it. So understanding the gaps between what a hiring manager requires and what you have to offer is critical. Even in a career change such as teaching, our parent will be competing against graduate intern-type applicants (who have many more years of future service to offer), and experienced hires. With trading in mind she will need to start to build her network and gain teaching experience in the penultimate year of her five-year action plan. This is because garnering knowledge and cultivating a network involves a considerable investment of time.

In Table 2.6 job seeker types have been matched with strengths and weaknesses. The transformer column details what you can do to counter any weaknesses that you may have because of your job seeker type.

Table 2.6 *Job seeker type transformer*

Job seeker type	Strengths	Weaknesses	Transformer tips
First jobber Trainee	Number of employment years that can be given	Lack of experience	Take part time or voluntary work. Enrol on work experience programmes.
		Lack of knowledge	Build professional network and read sector news.
		Lack of qualifications	Take further training.
Graduate intern	Number of employment years that can be given	Lack of experience	Take part time or voluntary work. Enrol on work experience programmes.

	Qualification attained	Lack of knowledge	Build professional network (stay in touch with fellow graduates) and read sector news
Second jobber Experienced hire	Experience in role or sector. General work experience, understanding corporate niceties.	May be perceived as stuck in your ways	Keep network current, read sector news, take relevant further training to demonstrate enthusiasm
Career changer	Experience in another sector or role = transferable skills. Established network.	Lack of experience	Join either: professional body, focus group, or pressure group for career change sector or role, or do part time or voluntary work in career change choice if possible
	General work experience, understanding corporate niceties	Lack of knowledge	Build network relevant to career change choice and read sector news
		Lack of qualifications	Take further training

We can see from Table 2.6 that the graduate interns and trainee/first jobbers are typified by similar strengths, weaknesses and transformer tips. One obstacle faced by both job seeker types is that when applying for their first job, they are usually competing against other graduates and school or college leavers. If you are a graduate intern or trainee first jobber, it is advisable not to leave it until the spring of your final year to apply for your first job. To maximize your chances of job seeking success, try developing at least one of the transformer tips in your final year of education.

Look for temporary off-peak graduate internships or work experience with chosen companies (such as PricewaterhouseCooper's LLP Summer Vacation Programme). When the summer comes you should be ahead of your competition.

The job seeker type that carries the most transformer tips is the career changer. This is because there is more risk associated with this job seeker type than any other. The risks are born out of the delay in career progression that a career change can cause. Even after a career changer finds employment in his or her new career choice, he or she may suffer a reduction in income at the career change stage and on through the first new role phase.

Once career changers have gained some experience (18 months plus) they are ostensibly second jobbers. This job seeker type carries the least risk and represents a chronological career progression. Career changers should focus on the value of previous work experience that they can bring to new roles. Most have amassed organizational, communication and people skills, all of which are transferable because they can be utilized in any role, and hugely benefit the employer. However, transferable skills alone may not satisfy prospective employers' recruitment needs. At a time when the unemployment rate is low, 5.2 per cent at the time of writing (http://www.statistics.gov.uk, January 2003), hiring managers will seek to reduce the risks of recruiting. It is safer for them to hire second jobbers or graduate interns. These job seeker types either already have sector or occupational experience, or are amply qualified for the role.

In Chapter 3 the emphasis is on being a 'buyer', as opposed to a 'seller', in your career of choice. As a buyer you should be able to convince recruiters that you are a low risk employee regardless of the type of job seeker that you are. Buyers know what price to pay for a purchase. They accrue their bottom and top line wisdom through studying their market. So the next chapter hones in on how to research your market or career of choice. There is an emphasis on recognizing new or evolving roles, the job seeker's equivalent of gaps in the market, where there is likely to be a demand. In being a buyer you should ensure that you are able to reap the benefits of the hidden jobs market, and to maximize every job opportunity that you uncover.

3 | Be a buyer in a sellers' market

When thinking about our current employment most of us are primarily concerned with internal influences. Do we get on with our boss? How can we shorten our working day? This is probably because we have greater control over internal influences than we do over external ones. The employment market, however, is largely driven by external factors. A downturn in the economy is likely to lead to redundancies, evolution of current roles, or downsizing. Conversely an upturn in the economy or emergence of a new market, such as new media, creates new job opportunities. As at the present when unemployment is at a low rate, because people tend to change jobs less, job opportunities are scarce. This means that most candidates are sellers in a buyers' market, the buyers being prospective employers.

In such a climate recruiters can make very low risk employment decisions. They can choose experienced hires, people who have been working in the same sector or role for several years. This is not as easily achieved where demand outstrips supply, where there is a skills shortage, an emerging market exists, or the employer has difficulty attracting calibre candidates. So in order to turn the tables and become a buyer in a sellers' market, we need to understand what is driving our prospective employer's recruitment needs. This involves understanding our prospective employer's market, or in other words the industry.

FIND A GAP IN THE MARKET

In Chapter 1 it was suggested that you could find out about different roles through referring to *The Occupations Year Book*, realistic job previews, and prospective employers' Web sites and job vacancy advertisements. This is a useful way of obtaining information to support your career path decisions. In addition, through conducting this type of desk research you can begin to amass industry news and information about your career of choice. As well as researching job markets in these ways, you could use industry news or financial market Internet sites to garner information.

Print media research

You will find company 'year books' in the reference section of your local library. The books are segmented in various ways: generally by company sector, or by turnover, as in *The Times Top 1000* and *Fortune 1000 Companies* published by Kompass.

If you perform an expert role such as human resources management, sales or marketing, you may prefer to read role rather than industry specific news. This will depend on the influence that the sector in which you work has on your role. There are many publications giving industry and role specific news, some free on subscription though most are paid for.

If you prefer life stories and would rather read about the practice than the theory, try reading executive biographies and business success stories about your chosen sector or role. Books such as these are often a great source of inspiration and real life career tips.

You could also read about business failures, to learn from others' mistakes and increase your understanding of threats to your chosen industry. Try *Boo Hoo: A dot com story* for a little alternative guidance therapy. There are suggested executive biographies and business histories in the Bibliography of Appendix 1.

Online research

The Internet is one of the most powerful research tools at your disposal. Industry specific news can be updated dynamically online, much like breaking news on live television. How you approach your Internet search depends on what you want to find out.

If you want to research a specific company whose name you know, you can either use an Internet search engine such as http://www.google.co.uk or a company's search engine such as http://hoovers.com (see Appendix 1 for a full list). Do not assume that if you know the company name the company URL will be something like http://COMPANYNAME.com. Surprisingly even Fortune 1000 companies do not always have intuitive URLs. If the company is part of a larger group you may have difficulty finding your target company, the subsidiary, unless you use a search engine. You can also use search engines to find press releases on people, products and companies.

When you have found the company's Web site, go to the 'about us' section. This will normally give you the company history, size, turnover details and possibly management structure. Watch out for how the company is described, as this will give you an insight into its corporate culture. If there is a FAQ (frequently asked questions) section, read it and get to know its contents: it should describe what the company does in a clear, logical way. Check 'press' or 'news' for information about new products or services, and any new appointments. Customer case studies and client testimonials give a valuable insight into what the company provides for customers, and also what it is proud of. In addition, case studies may indicate what products or services a company is investing resources in. When reading this section, think about how you could help the company satisfy its customers and outperform its competitors. Read executive biographies to glean what type of people work for the company and whether there are personal development opportunities within the company. Watch out for chances to chat to line managers or existing employees; some companies provide online chat forums or e-mail addresses of employees.

If you want to access general business trend and forecast news, or to develop industry specific knowledge, you can again use the Internet to gather information. For a list of industry specific news sites and business trends analysis sites see Appendix 1.

GRADUATES' MARKET STALL

If you are a graduate job seeker, one of your biggest challenges is differentiation. This is because graduate recruitment is mostly seasonal. Ordinarily you will be competing against a large volume of peers for a small number of jobs, so you need to set your stall out in such a way as to head off any similar competition. If you are competing with graduates with the same or possibly better grades than you, you need to have something extra on offer to gain a competitive advantage. This is where transformer tips (see Table 2.6) can help. If you can demonstrate that you have developed expertise through work experience, voluntary work, industry newsmongering or networking, you will have an edge over your peers. This businesslike approach to your career should impress your prospective employers. You are more likely to be recruited if you can show initiative in this way. For a full list of graduate sites with details of internships and work experience schemes, see Appendix 1.

As well as advertising graduate placements, many organizations exhibit at the National Graduate Recruitment Fair. This annual fair is sponsored by the Guardian Media Group. Graduates can talk directly to prospective employers and gain a full understanding of career prospects within organizations. You can view an exhibitors list online (http://www.gradjobs.co.uk) and research your target companies from there. If you decide to attend you should set SMART objectives to ensure that your time is used productively. Treat the fair like your first day at work: dress smartly and take enough copies of your CV for each prospective employer that you plan to meet. You should also take a notepad and keep a log of who you talk to and what they say about their organizations. Try to collect their business cards, and where possible arrange further interviews. Also prepare to be interviewed on the spot.

RESEARCH FOR A PURPOSE

You will have realized that there is a plethora of company information available to you. Ultimately your goal is to identify a gap in the market, where demand outstrips supply and there is an opportunity for you to fill the gap. This is easily accomplished when you understand what recruitment needs exist in your sector.

Economics and the employment market are largely driven by external change, which means that most employment trends are in response to the environment. For example, a worldwide decline in the value of technology stocks led many investment banks to make technology stock analysts redundant during 2002.

Monitoring environmental change allows companies and organizations to forecast what resources they will need to ensure success *now* and in the *future*. One way to predict recruitment demand is to be alert to the external changes that are affecting your sector of choice. As employees are most companies' largest resource, if you understand the environmental changes you too may be able to anticipate growing or emerging recruitment demands.

EMPLOYMENT MARKETS LOWDOWN

Through increased awareness of our environment we can make calculated career moves into roles where demand is high or growing. To gain an insight into recruitment needs we interviewed recruiters from some of the UK's most successful companies about recent environmental changes and their impact on hiring demands.

Inside temporary recruitment

Janet McGlaughlin is the Operations Director of Pertemps Recruitment Partnership (http://www.pertemps.co.uk), a national recruitment consultancy with over 200 UK offices. Pertemps employs over 1,500 staff and payrolls in excess of 30,000 temporary personnel a week, supplying a broad range of job category staff to top FTSE 100 companies.

What employment trend changes have you noticed over the past two to three years?

There has been an outsourcing call centre boom. Services such as helpdesk facilities, marketing, sales and customer service are now invariably handled via a call centre. Examples of industry sectors that have included the call centre function in their business strategies are hospitality and leisure, financial and insurance services, utilities, and of late health services and councils have also made investments in this area.

The public sector, in responding to increased competition, legislative changes and customer charters, is creating recruitment demands. While manufacturing has been affected in certain geographical locations, we have not seen a vast difference in recruitment demands in the north east.

Recruitment requirements in both the IT and telecommunications sector have been reduced. Though both have reached a level of market saturation in terms of hardware, software developments and upgrades are still creating IT recruitment demands, and the mobile telecommunications sector product diversifications such as picture messaging and broadband are also creating demand.

Legislative changes in the last decade have discouraged employers from discriminating during the selection process, and these changes have forced them to adhere to equal opportunities employment practices. This has led to broader employment remits, which have seen increased diversity in the workplace. Good examples of these changes are employers' attitude to employing more mature candidates (50 plus), providing facilities for employees with disabilities and improving flexible working hours for those employees with young families or dependants.

Further changes can be seen in the profile of candidates. Most roles have been expanded, so candidates now have to multitask and use a number of skills within their working day. Additionally, recent employment legislation has seen a change in the relationship between the worker and the employer. Workers are more aware than ever of their rights, and have come to expect that employers will offer skill and career development, equal rights and adherence to health and safety at work; and that they will also offer work–life balance, and that conditions in the working environment do not cause stress. There has been a significant increase in stress related illnesses, and employers are becoming aware of their responsibilities.

The Agency Worker Directive, which may come into force in late 2003, will have a huge impact on recruitment consultancies. The Directive will align working conditions for temporary workers with those of permanent employees. This means that temporary workers will receive, for example, the same training, pay rates, holiday and pension benefits as permanent employees. As more and more agencies permanently employ temporary workers to fill long-term assignments with their client companies, agencies will now have to offer similar terms to their workers as corporates do to their employees. This must then be reflected in the charges that agencies make to the client.

How have recruitment consultancies reacted to these changes?

The Agency Directive should attract new candidates into the temporary employment market. The potential increased cost of hiring staff on a temporary basis means that clients will have a higher expectation, and agencies must be prepared to make an investment. More agencies are now offering free training to enhance the existing skills of their workers, in order to ensure that client companies are engaging staff who can be productive from day one. We have been actively doing this for quite some time.

Pertemps is very committed to investing in its people, and as an accredited IIP (Investors in People) Company and NVQ trainer we are one of the largest suppliers of training to businesses in the UK. We are able, through the New Deal programme, to secure government funding to train our temps where development needs arise. Not only are we able to train our clients' employees, we are also able to offer NVQ training to our temporary workers, ensuring consistent quality and productivity irrespective of employment status. In addition we have the highest number of professionally qualified consultants by examination within the UK.

What sectors are still employing IT and accountancy professionals?

These professional roles are always sought after, but if candidates are finding that job opportunities are in short supply they should consider working in a different sector or perhaps making a lateral career move.

What new roles have you seen emerge over the past two to three years?

Many traditional roles have evolved or emerged to encompass an online function. And there is a growing prevalence of service provision via call centres.

What future challenges do recruitment consultancies face?

We face legislative changes that will have a huge impact on the way in which temps work in the UK. These legislative changes will transform many recruitment agencies into permanent employers of staff that temp for corporates. Agencies therefore will be equally liable under employment law as corporate employers are now.

Recruitment consultants will have to keep abreast of legislative changes and assess candidates according to the client's employee requirements. Consultants now partner with clients to ensure that they fully understand what their requirements are. This has led to an elevation of the recruitment consultant's role in the hiring process. It has also resulted in greater investment from consultants and their agencies in consultants' training and personal development.

Inside contract catering

Mike Stapleton is the Corporate Affairs Manager for the Compass Group (http://www.compass-group.com) in the UK and Ireland. The Compass Group is the world's largest contract foodservice company, with annual revenue in excess of £10 billion. Compass Group has over 375,000 employees working in over 100 countries around the world.

Ten billion pounds in revenue is a huge figure. What sorts of businesses use food services?

There is a general trend for businesses to contract out, or outsource, services that are not their core business. Compass Group has 26 sector-specific operating companies, all of which specialize in different sector needs. As well as geographic differences in tastes and cultural needs, our sector specialists allow us to cater for the specific and very varied requirements of people in the workplace, railway stations, airports, fine dining, universities, schools, healthcare institutions, offshore and remote sites, retail stores, motorways, sporting events and shopping malls.

For example, Scolarest provides food service for students of all ages from nursery pupils through to university undergraduates. The requirements of the education market include the need for healthy eating and the provision of well-balanced food served in a caring but very fashionable manner. There is currently a focus, in this sector, on innovation to encourage healthy eating. The specialization is quite different within Eurest executive dining, where fine dining and corporate hospitality are provided for clients such as Goldman Sachs, Morgan Stanley and the Institute of Directors.

How have recent events in the City affected the Compass Group?

Many corporate clients have downsized considerably recently. Obviously there are less people, therefore, eating our food. However, the public sector is currently a buoyant market, particularly in healthcare and education. These sectors have customer charters to meet, which are timelined, so they are tending to outsource food service provision and are therefore fuelling demand for food and hospitality services.

Contracting out facilities in both the private and public sectors is very much in vogue globally. Recent downsizing in many financial service sectors is counteracted by more contracts being on offer from other sectors. The forecast for this over the next few years is very encouraging.

The hospitality sector was hard hit by 11 September 2001 and foot-and-mouth disease. What has been the impact for your business?

As our business is contract and retail based, we are not solely reliant upon tourism for new or continued business. Whereas consumers can quickly cancel hotel reservations or change holiday locations in response to global unrest, people's work and shopping habits are more predictable and stable. So the contract food service industry is less susceptible to immediate changing consumer demand than the hotel and tourism sectors. Worldwide estimates indicate that the total global contract food service market is worth over £170 billion. Less than 30 per cent of this market is currently contracted out, so the market is a robust and growing one.

How does the work in contract food service provision differ from working in a restaurant or a bar?

The main difference is the hours of work. When our employees provide food to businesses and industry it is usually during office hours. A typical working day for an employee starts at around 8.00 am and finishes at around 5.00 pm. Employees of restaurants, bars or hotels usually find that they are working while everyone else is socializing, and more often than not, split shifts are involved.

Contract food service provision also takes employees off high streets and into leisure centres, shopping malls, the workplace, schools and hospitals. If the food service provider is a large corporation, such as we are, employees may find that they can relocate and remain with the same company. This is actively encouraged by the Compass Group, not just nationally but often internationally.

In addition to catering roles, what other occupations might a candidate expect to find within a contract food service provision organization?

It may depend on the size of the organization, but at Compass Group, for example, we have sales and marketing, procurement, finance, HR and training, legal and large operations departments. We recruit at all levels. Candidates entering the industry with no qualifications or experience may join our Modern Apprenticeship Schemes or in-house development programmes. Candidates entering with existing qualifications or experience will often enter into supervisory, graduate management development, chef's development, general and specialist management, or executive appointments. Most of the programmes are based on a 'career path' ethos, where candidates can gain on and off-job experience in operational, supervisory and management roles.

What future challenges does the contract food service market face?

In the UK we have had a very low birth rate in recent years and a low unemployment rate, which means that most businesses are trying to recruit from an ever-shrinking pool of candidates. In order to counter this we are focusing on retaining our staff, as are most forward-thinking businesses.

We do this primarily by encouraging employees to develop career paths within the Group. We also support employee relocation, and will endeavour to accommodate employees within the Group in the event that an employee needs to move. In addition we help employees who prefer home working through financing SOHOs (small office home offices) and following flexible working practices where appropriate.

We recently created and filled a new role in the form of a Recruitment and Retention Director. The prime focus is issues such as these, as well as the development of processes like succession planning. We firmly believe that staff retention will help us to secure our future and the future of the contract food service market as a whole. Retention of great people also makes consistency of high standards, a USP of ours, a lot easier.

Hospitality has not been perceived as a strong career option in the past. Furthermore the contract food service market is perceived as one of the least glamorous sectors within the hospitality industry. In fact Compass Group was founded in 1941 as Factory Canteens Limited to feed munitions workers who were legally entitled to one hot meal a day, and the history of our sector is very much entrenched in this canteen culture. Yet, for example, we provide the catering for the Formula One British Grand Prix at Silverstone.

The contract food service sector has some work to do in raising public awareness of this and attracting new recruits into the sector. In recognition of this we have partnered with Springboard (http://www.springboard.co.uk), a careers organization for 14 to 18-year-olds, and we have developed our own electronic recruitment site (http://jobsat-compass.co.uk), and an in-house recruitment agency with national offices. Our advertising and communications activity has considerably increased, and we work very hard at providing standards, which lead to client referrals.

As technological advances are made in food preparation and distribution processes the contract food service market must continue to progress in tandem with them. Compass is very much the pioneer in this respect. A clear focus on operational excellence, in particular supply chain management and operational innovation, should ensure continually high standards.

Harnessing the advantages of these changes is a challenge to most businesses. At Compass Group we foster a knowledge-sharing environment where sector-specific expertise is pooled centrally. We have done this to avoid duplicating work and ensure a consistently high operational standard. Maintaining a high level of operating quality is therefore a day-to-day challenge for the contract food service market.

Inside construction

Tony Welch is the HR Director of Galliford Try plc (http://www.gallifordtry.plc.uk), a national commercial construction and house building company. Galliford Try is one of the UK's top 15 national construction contractors (*Building Magazine,* 19 July 2002), employing 2,200 people with an annual turnover in excess of £650 million. Tony Welch also chairs the Construction Confederation Training Committee and the Construction Industry's Joint Council, which negotiates with trade unions to promote positive industrial relations and improved health and safety standards.

What changes have impacted the construction sector over the past two to three years?

The government has initiated several changes, for example the introduction of PFI (private finance initiatives) has affected the education and healthcare sectors. PFI is similar to a hire purchase scheme whereby education and healthcare institutions may seek private funding for projects, which the government then pays back to investors over an agreed period of time. PFI has therefore released new sources of cash to these public sector institutions, which in turn has created a demand for new and regenerative construction work.

Another government initiative is Frame Work Agreements (FWAs). These projects have a different mandate to traditional construction projects in that they are long term. An FWA usually lasts for about four to five years and incorporates designing, financing, building, maintaining and maintenance contingency plans for a site. As an FWA's duration is longer, financing of the project can also be spread over the full FWA term. This means that clients are increasingly involved in the cost control and profitability of projects.

There has also been a growing focus on health and safety practices. The Major Contractor's Group Safety Charter requires that by 2003 all construction employees will be a fully qualified work force, not just in terms of technical skills but also in terms of prerequisite health and safety qualifications.

We have a national housing shortage, and exponents like Ken Livingstone (Mayor of London 2003) and John Prescott (Labour Party Deputy Prime Minister 2003) are changing local and central government policy to enable brownfield (urban or industrialized areas) regeneration, so as to create affordable housing. As a result housing associations are generating demand for brownfield construction work.

The mobile communications sector is creating an increasing demand for specialist construction services. With the advent of third generation (3G) technology, there are sector requirements for masts, switching centres and cell site constructions. Sourcing suitable locations to extend mobile phone signals networks, and erecting masts on these sites, has been and continues to be a necessity for this sector.

How has work changed in the contract construction sector in the light of these changes?

The main change, which has permeated throughout, is an adoption of a partnership, relationship-building approach to projects. This has meant that contract construction companies get involved with the end user (for example, the teacher who will work in a newly refurbished school) far earlier on than they used to. If we look at education PFI projects, construction contractors are now involved in the first meetings with teachers and local education authorities, where different clients' needs must be understood and consolidated into a project plan. In addition the contract construction industry's role has evolved beyond

GallifordTry

If you're building a career, choose an employer who'll be committed to you: GallifordTry

Fast growing and forward thinking, Galliford Try is one of the UK's top 15 construction contractors. We're a key voice in the industry; backing training initiatives, supporting improved standards, and committed to new ways of working.

Our biggest strength is people: we believe in harnessing individual talent in group projects, encouraging ongoing learning and sharing knowledge and techniques for mutual benefit. That's an unusual attitude in an industry often perceived as old-fashioned, but it's an outlook that pays off: our groundbreaking approach to training has received four National Training Awards (including the Special Award).

We're involved in some of the UK's most exciting building projects, from a Lord Rogers-designed retail village in Kent, to Birmingham's Millennium Point, and the All England Lawn Tennis Club at Wimbledon. And around the country, you'll see us active in a diverse range of building programmes in the public and private sectors, working in partnership with clients and building users to ensure that we always create what people need.

The business is structured to offer the best possible support: to clients, and to our people. Within Galliford Try, different specialisms have their own dedicated teams. We have particular expertise in construction for the communication sector, for instance, and operate several prestige names in housebuilding. All of that means excellent career opportunities for people joining Galliford Try: we're actively committed to your long term development.

Graduates can join our construction operations and benefit from a three-year training that will lead to certification by the Institute of Civil Engineering, Royal Institute of Quantity Surveyors, or Chartered Institute of Building. We also offer opportunities to people with other qualifications and expertise: marketing, finance, and IT for example. Whatever your career path with us, you're assured of individual attention and consideration: the emphasis is on your skills and ambitions. We're equally attentive when it comes to salary and benefits packages.

Please send a CV to: Hazel Deakin, Training and Personnel Officer Galliford Try, Wolvey, Hinckley, Leicestershire LE10 3JH. Email: hazel.deakin@gallifordtry.co.uk

We are an equal opportunities employer

just building premises to maintaining and cleaning them. This early involvement means that contract construction companies are now in a position to influence design, financing and budget allocation through direct negotiation with the end user. Whereas before designers and architects would contract building work out to construction companies, now construction companies contract the designers.

The contract construction sector has reacted to the government tightening of safety programmes through raising the standard of qualification levels for site staff. For example all operatives and staff working on Heathrow Terminal 5 have an appropriate NVQ and they have passed safety tests.

Which sectors are creating the most demand?

Public sectors such as education, healthcare and housing associations. The transport, industry and utilities sectors are also creating demand, as are the retail, leisure and mobile communications sectors. It is not the case that one sector alone creates more demand than another, because one retail contract may be far bigger than several other sector contracts. For example the outlet centre near Ashford in Kent designed by Lord Rogers was a £23 million project. Galliford Try was behind the construction of this site, which is one of the largest designer outlet villages outside of the United States.

There has been a lot of recent (Christmas 2002) coverage in the press of skills shortages in the construction sector. Why is this the case?

Operative or site management work in the contract construction sector can be arduous, it involves long and unsociable hours, and there is often a requirement to travel to different sites. In contrast, service industry office or call centre work is less physically demanding. Attitudes towards skilled labour professions have not been good for the past decade or so, and we have experienced a reduction in the number of young people, 16 to 18-year-olds, coming into the industry.

Second to this, the system for funding training within the contract construction industry dates back to the 1960s. Applying for training grants is a long, convoluted procedure which puts off many smaller contractor companies.

In addition the profit margins within the contract construction sector are slim, so if a company is not generating enough revenue it tends to cut its training spend. The construction industry was in decline during the mid to late 1990s, and many companies reduced their training investment. These three factors combined have compounded skills shortages within the industry.

What new roles have emerged in the construction sector?

At Galliford Try we have seen the emergence of service and mainte-nance, and facilities management roles. This has largely been brought about by the growing remit of PFI projects. Software packages are now relied on heavily by project managers for planning, budget forecasting and design purposes. This has meant that the project manager's skill set has broadened.

Due to pressing government demands to increase health and safety working practices, the prevalence of trainers and HR staff is growing. At Galliford Try for example we have developed health and safety courses with the Institute of Health and Safety, which are aligned to NVQ levels. The courses are examined, and certificates and safety cards (for use on sites) are awarded to those that pass. We have also developed a health and safety refresher course so that, rather like First Aid refreshers, employees' health and safety knowledge is continually updated and of a high standard. The construction skills safety scheme is a basic standard, and was not aligned to specific qualifications or the different safety responsibilities that supervisory roles encompass, which is why we developed refresher and qualification-aligned health and safety courses.

What are the future challenges for the construction sector?

As a partnership approach to contract construction is becoming more common, employees will need to continue to develop communication skills. Our project managers are now called upon to secure buy-in from budget holders, influencers and decision makers, to negotiate with designers, subcontractors and facilities managers, and to keep end users informed of progress.

The industry must invest in its people. We expect that clients will demand higher standards of work in the future, and we are already experiencing skills shortages in some roles.

We are finding that the entry-level age for the sector has increased. We have received applications from candidates in their 20s who want to career change. We need to continue this trend and attract 16 and 18-year-olds into apprenticeship schemes.

The DTI (Department of Trade and Industry) launched a Construction Best Practice Programme in 1998, the objective of which is to encourage industry-wide adoption of best practices. In accordance with this programme, we need to ensure that knowledge transfer and knowledge management are actively encouraged. Many contractors fear sharing their 'trade secrets' with their competitors. We get around the 'trade secrets' conflict of interests by talking about our experiences, or what we have done. It is only through knowledge transfer that we will develop as an industry, avoid duplication of the same (invariably) costly mistakes, and continue to increase the standard of construction in the UK. At Galliford Try we encourage our employees, on all levels, to pool their knowledge.

Inside food and drink manufacturing

Barbara Firth is the York site Recruitment Manager for Nestlé UK (http://www.nestle.co.uk). Nestlé is the world's largest food and drink manufacturing company, employing 230,000 people all over the world. In the UK Nestlé employs approximately 10,000 staff. Nestlé manufactures well-known brands such as Buitoni, Perrier, Nescafé, Ski yoghurts and Kit Kat.

What recent market changes have affected the food and drink manufacturing industry?

The changes vary across food and drink manufacturing businesses, but can involve anything from environmental and legislative changes to new developments in food science. At Nestlé we constantly respond to a variety of market changes every day due to the fast-moving nature of the industry we work in.

What are typical roles within the food and drink manufacturing sector?

Food and drink manufacturing is very much a market-led industry. The marketing function is very strong within Nestlé UK. Along with most other large corporate companies, Nestlé employs people in core business functions on sites and at our head offices. Traditional roles might include IT, technical support, customer service, marketing, research and development, product development and sales. A proportion of employees in the industry work in our factories in roles such as production, management, scientific development and engineering.

For example, we house the Nestlé Worldwide Centre of Excellence for Confectionery Research at our Nestlé Rowntree site in York. We develop new products in the Centre for the UK and other Nestlé markets abroad.

We also develop new manufacturing processes and techniques that are compatible with the requirements of different countries.

Another key business function within the food and drink manufacturing sector is supply chain management. We have to ensure that our customers and consumers get the food and drink that they want in perfect condition and when they want it. We work very closely with our customers in managing the supply chain for them. Our customers include:

- major multiples such as Tesco, Sainsbury and Asda and other major supermarkets;
- multiple impulse vendors such as Boots, W H Smith and garage forecourts;
- wholesalers and cash and carry stores such as Palmer and Harvey, Makro and Booker.

What are the entry-level qualifications for the food and drink manufacturing industry?

For office and factory roles we would expect a good standard of general education: five GCSEs at grade C and above. We recruit candidates into Modern Apprenticeship Schemes and train them for two years to an NVQ Level 3 standard.

We do not have a formal graduate development recruitment programme; however, we actively recruit graduates into specific management roles, and as with non-graduates, we provide an extensive infrastructure to support individuals' personal development through their chosen career path. We aim to recruit graduate calibre candidates into all our management roles, but it is not a mandatory requirement that managers are degree qualified. It is more important that qualifications, skills and experience are appropriate to the job that the candidate is applying for.

What future challenges does the food and drink manufacturing industry face?

As our products are market and trend led, the industry needs to continue to invest in product development and quality management. At Nestlé UK we have started to group or categorize our products differently so that we can respond quickly to the changing demands of the consumer market and understand their tastes and preferences. For example one of our categories deals with the 'eat later' market, and examines all the snacks that consumers are likely to purchase to eat later, with a focus on delivering those products to consumers when they want them.

Customers are more demanding now than they used to be, with major multiples developing 'own brands'. This puts pressure on the industry to develop more cost effective manufacturing processes and continually retain the value of the brands that it manufactures.

Consumer tastes change rapidly. For example, pre-selected boxed chocolates used to be a popular gift. However, consumers today want a greater level of choice: they want to be able to pick and mix what goes in the box.

Consumers also want to understand the nutritional content of their food and drink. We have responded to this need at Nestlé UK by featuring nutritional information on our sites and food packaging. We also sponsor and conduct major nutritional research across the globe (visit http://www.nestle.co.uk/nutrition/checkyourdiet/checkyourdiet.asp for further information).

Consumers are also tending to eat away from home more. We have reacted to this shift by developing our vending machine range of products and the way in which products are packaged. They may also purchase items to consume later, so we want to ensure that the product is as good to eat in five minutes as it is at the time of purchase. We have also opened several Nescafé cafes in response to this eating out trend.

Inside investment banking

UBS Warburg (http://www.ubswarburg.com) operates globally as a client-driven investment banking and securities firm. UBS Warburg employs 17,000 individuals in 30 countries around the world, providing product innovation, top quality research and advice, and complete access to the world's capital markets. UBS Warburg was recently named 'Bank of the Year' (*Investment Dealer's Digest*, a leading US publication, 2002) and was listed as a *Times* Top 100 Employer of Choice (2002).

What major changes have impacted the investment banking sector over the past two to three years?

Recruitment has changed significantly in the last two years within investment banking, partly as a result of current market conditions. Market volatility has meant a decline in overall recruitment; however, UBS Warburg has still continued to recruit during this time.

We have also seen a shift towards recruiting both directly and online, which we have used successfully within graduate recruitment for some time (see http://www.ubs.com/e/careers_candidates.html). UBS Warburg has developed a Web site to promote the working environment and give

Robin Schoenman / Equity Trading / Stamford

Global career opportunities

UBS Investment Bank is a leading global securities and investment banking firm, providing a full spectrum of products to institutional and corporate clients, intermediaries, governments and hedge funds worldwide. UBS Investment Bank is a business group of UBS AG, which is listed on the New York, Tokyo and Swiss stock exchanges.

It's true that building a career in financial services is a demanding option. You'll need a strong personality, an ability to learn and think quickly and the determination to excel. The return on your investment will be a truly rewarding career and outstanding opportunities.

With over 70,000 people delivering our outstanding services and products in 50 countries, UBS Investment Bank is looking for individuals from different backgrounds - with a range of perspectives, experiences and skills - to reflect the depth and breadth of our client base.

Now is the time to take your first steps towards a great future.

All applications to be made on line.

If you'd like to find out more:
www.ubs.com/investmentbank-careers

Diversity, one of our core values at UBS Investment Bank, is essential to our global success and that of our clients. To this end, we foster an innovative, flexible culture rooted in respect, ensuring that all talented UBS Investment Bank employees have the opportunity to thrive. As a result, we attract and retain open-minded, dedicated employees, each bringing a multitude of diverse perspectives to the firm.

By embracing diversity of cultures, skills and experiences, we create long-term value for our employees, clients and shareholders.

UBS Investment Bank

candidates an insight into the type of people we employ (see www.ubswarburg.com/careers). Candidates can read interviews with accountants and executive directors within investment banking. In addition all vacancies can be viewed online, and candidates can apply by posting their CVs to the site. This was unheard of two years ago when investment banks generally only advertised positions in the broadsheet press.

Have there been any emergent roles at UBS Warburg as a result of changing markets?

Information technology has revolutionized the financial services sector, and UBS Warburg is at the cutting edge of applying the technology essential to successful performance in this highly competitive industry. Traditional constraints on our business such as time, distance and the cost of delivery no longer apply. Now, one in five people at UBS Warburg are a technologist.

What career paths are available within investment banking?

UBS Warburg offers a wide range of job opportunities. It is not just about being an investment banker or a trader, we also have roles for secretaries, event coordinators, HR professionals, accountants, lawyers, business analysts, Web designers and technologists, and that's not an exhaustive list.

We recognize that the people joining us are looking for more than just a job – they are looking for challenging, rewarding, long-term careers in an organization that encourages them to continue developing their knowledge and skills, whatever their role may be. As an employer of choice we make great efforts to identify and recruit the top candidate for every role. We invest heavily in training and development.

UBS Warburg is a 'learning organization' with a history of significant investment in every individual's education and development, both technical and personal, throughout their career. We aim to deliver a comprehensive training framework that relates directly to transitions in an individual's career and their individual development needs.

Inside online grocery retail

Tesco.com is a recent addition to the Tesco portfolio (http://www.tesco.com); it was soft-launched in 1996 and hard-launched in 1999. John Browett is the Chief Executive Officer of Tesco.com, the online grocer for

Tesco. Tesco supermarket chain has 730 stores in the UK, operating in 10 countries with a total of over 979 stores internationally. Tesco employs 250,000 people worldwide, serving a population of 60 million in the UK and a total population of 280 million internationally.

During the last five years, Tesco has expanded from its traditional UK supermarket base into new countries, products and services. Tesco.com is now the world's leading online grocer.

Why was Tesco.com launched?

We introduced online shopping to our customers because they had always said that they thought the store was fantastic but could be better if we delivered to their homes. During the 1950s home deliveries were affordable for department stores and grocers. However, as the process was manual and labour costs were rising, home deliveries soon became too expensive for grocers to sustain.

The Internet made home delivery affordable because order capture and online payments are simply fully automated data feeds to local stores. Our customers pay for the cost of delivery, which is £5. We deliver to customers up to 25 minutes' driving time from their local store. Currently (January 2003) we cover 96.5 per cent of the UK population.

When was Tesco.com launched?

Our first delivery was in December 1996. This was the commencement of a two and a half year trial period. Tesco.com was launched properly in August 1999. By 2000 we had national coverage, and we found that Tesco.com was driving Internet uptake. Our customers valued online shopping so much they were buying PCs and gaining Internet access in order to enable this. In addition the growth of Tesco.com was positively correlated to the growth of e-commerce. And as the first online grocer we were at the forefront of a new industry (e-commerce).

How did you convert shopping at a store to online?

During the Tesco.com trial period we developed our online catalogue to replicate shopping in a store. At first we catalogued our goods online as we did for stock inventory and supply chain management control purposes. When a store is handling consumer goods, such as dairy products, the main focus is to store the goods at the right temperatures and sell stock ahead of its sell-by date. But customers don't shop like that, so we categorized our goods to reflect this. For example, if a customer wants to buy a banana today, he would enter '1' next to bananas. The site would present this information as both '1 banana' and '1kg [of] bananas', so that the customer could order either by the number or by the weight.

What are Tesco.com customers like?

Two-income households typify them in general, and most have children. About 80 per cent of our e-shoppers are female. It would not be accurate to describe our customers as affluent. For example, some customers who inhabit urban areas negate the need for a car or taxis by shopping online. A handful of customers who live in outlying communities, where the distance to the store exceeds 25 minutes' delivery time, have negotiated community collections from their nearest store and still grocery shop online.

How did the inception of the online grocery affect your supply chain management?

In principle it did not affect our supply chain, as the only change was to fully automate the process and feed data to local stores. As consumer goods shopping is seasonal in the main, there has been little supply impact on e-shopping.

What new roles emerged as a result?

Tesco.com created several new roles. They include 1,600–1,800 van drivers, 4,500 personal shoppers (staff to prepare online orders), dot.com section managers (responsible for managing online order fulfilment in-store), Web developers, online marketeers, in-store promotions managers, Web editors and Web affiliate managers.

What other aspects of the Tesco.com site were developed as a result of consumers shopping online?

We have taken the Tesco Clubcard (a customer loyalty card where one point is gained for every pound spent with Tesco) online. Customers can register for a Clubcard online and also register to receive e-vouchers.

We provide financial services such as loans, credit cards, and house, pet and car insurance through Tesco Personal Finance. About 20 per cent of our financial services sold to date have been acquired online. We have developed localized online communities that are centred around the store. In-store promotions mirror this decentralized approach by being driven by local consumer demand. We have also developed

Ringtone
or
vibrate?

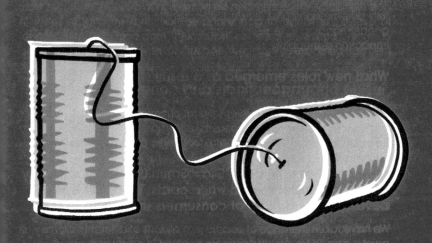

**It's time to make decisions
that really matter...**

www.tesco.com/graduates

a Baby and Toddler Club site where mothers can chat to other parents and share parenting tips. We have found that today's parents are information hungry, and want to research baby and toddler products, car seats and push chairs and so on before they buy. Our Healthy Living site is another example of a consumer-driven online community where shoppers can access the latest nutritional information.

What are the future challenges for online grocers?

We need to continue to listen to our customers and deliver what they want to them. As broadband uptake grows, we hope to continually improve the e-shopping experience, making it faster and therefore increasing the efficiency of the service.

We are retaining our market leader position by expanding Tesco.com into different countries and developing e-shopping technology. Tesco.com is now in Korea, the Republic of Ireland and the United States (in the form of a joint venture with Safeway Inc).

We constantly look to improve working practice to achieve greater cost efficiency, which can then be passed on to our customers. We want to evolve the range of goods and services that we offer in line with changing consumer tastes, so that should Tesco.com customers wish to, they can purchase all that they need without having to leave their homes.

Inside pharmaceuticals and consumer healthcare

GlaxoSmithKline (GSK) is an international pharmaceutical and consumer healthcare company. Its global quest is to improve the quality of human life by enabling people to do more, feel better and live longer.

When most people hear 'GlaxoSmithKline' they probably think of laboratories and white coats. What is the work like at GSK?

We employ a wide range of people with all sorts of different skills, as well as scientists. There's a long process involved in producing pharmaceuticals. Discovering and producing new medicines begins with research and development. New medicines are tested extensively before they are ready to be used by patients. We also develop manufacturing systems and processes, and establish supply networks.

When a product is approved for use, other areas of our business get to work. For example we have large marketing, sales and procurement departments. We have a finance department, which supports the business

---

in general. We also have a large IT department that provides support to ensure manufacturing quality management, supply chain management, systems support, corporate site and e-business development.

So candidates could consider job hunting outside their sector with a company like GSK if they are, say, marketeers or IT professionals?

Absolutely. We have, for example, a major consumer marketing function including Ribena, Lucozade, Aquafresh, Horlicks and many other well-known brands that are sold in supermarkets and shops. Core roles such as accountancy, IT, marketing, HR and sales are still very much in demand in large businesses like GSK. We also employ legal professionals because our pharmaceutical products are patented, and this team plays an important part in protecting our intellectual property.

We would encourage candidates to look outside of their industry, if it is in decline as the new media and investment banking sectors have been, or if their promotional prospects are slight, to more traditional sectors. It's important for candidates to match what makes them happy in their work with the culture of the organization. For example at GSK we promote and support self-led development. This is great for innovators and free thinkers who want to be valued for what they contribute. We are a diverse employer, and as such support the employment of disabled people. We are very much about empowering the individual employee.

We are aware of our social responsibility to world health and have many different activities that address health issues in developing countries. We are heavily involved in the Global Alliance to Eliminate Lymphatic Filariasis, a 20-year programme to eradicate one of the world's most disfiguring and disabling diseases. On a more local scale we support employees in the UK who are 'Making a Difference' in their own communities. Through the scheme, staff are able to apply for funding for charity or community organizations that they are directly involved with.

SUMMARY

Understanding your employability worth should have whet your job hunting appetite. In the next chapter we get to grips with techniques to snare the most elusive of jobs.

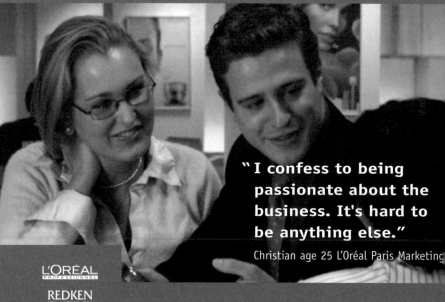

Hunt jobs down

Sit down for this next statistic: it is estimated that only about one-third of jobs are advertised. That leaves a two-thirds subversive majority to be found and snared. This would lead most to inquire what the majority is made up of, as understanding this could unlock access to the largest jobs market.

It can be explained in part as follows. Most HR professionals and line managers consider it good practice to fill a job internally if they can. Some have access to an intranet system where they can post their own vacancies, others may rely on e-mail or word of mouth. So if a situation becomes vacant within an organization, departmental staff at least are likely to hear of it. They could recommend a friend (networking) or consider other applicants (previous or current speculative applications). Or the company's hiring manager could contact a headhunter. In this way the job is filled before it is ever advertised.

So in order to tap into the hidden jobs market you need to:

☐ Recognize new or evolving roles that you could fulfil, either within your current organization or in a new one. Be the supply that fills the demand.
☐ Network.
☐ Apply for jobs speculatively.

If you are not frightened or confused by the concept of asking a complete stranger for a job, give yourself a huge pat on the back. Most of us are petrified by it. So to enable us to conquer our inhibitions or hone our speculative job-seeking skills, there follows an interview with a networking guru, and a discussion with a career management luminary, to shed light on the hidden jobs market.

NETWORKING

Ask an expert

Flemming Madsen is a co-founder of Powermingle Ltd, an Internet matching company that helps people to extend their professional networks. Flemming used to work in the electronic manufacturing sector. When attending conferences and exhibitions, he found that his ability to build his network was limited by chance. There was no way of recognizing new business acquaintances that he could either help or seek help from. Frustrated by this ineffective use of prime networking time, Flemming decided to develop networking matching software. http://www.powermingle.com was devised for professional individuals who wish to grow their networks. 'Mingle zones' were designed for event and conference attendees, so that individuals could ring-fence those professionals they wished to network with.

What is networking?

Networking is a system for building up acquaintances in an area that you are interested in. Though it's usually associated with work, you could network to further an ambition or hobby that you have. It's about building and extending relationships where either you can help someone else, or he or she can help you. It's not about finding prospective customers, or having a Rolodex the size of the London Eye on your desk.

Why network?

There are three main benefits to networking. First, working life has changed an awful lot over the past 10 to 20 years. Whereas people could expect to be employed by one company, or at least fulfil one role in their career, now they are subjected to frequent change. This means that they are forced to manage their own careers. Jobs are more or less temporary now, so everybody is in the business of building their own career. Getting a job through referral is the most common way that people get jobs. If your network is small and contains mostly friends and family with few acquaintances, you are less likely to be personally recommended for a job.

Second, we all need help and advice from professionals at times. It doesn't matter what type of advice you need, none of us are expert at everything. Whether it's a plumber or a lawyer that you need, if you already knew one, you'd call them up and ask for their advice. It is only when you don't know one that you have to get out the Yellow Pages or visit yell.com. Once you have found your expert you then have to validate his or her advice or services. All of this takes time and carries an element of risk. So a good network can save time and money.

Third, if you think of yourself as a product, like an exhibitor's stand at a conference, you cannot afford to miss a conference that all of your competitors are attending. It's important to be seen at the same events so that everybody takes you as seriously as your competitors. This means that when your advice or services are needed, you will be at the forefront of your associates' minds.

How do you start to build up a network?

If you don't have a Rolodex or heap of business cards, start with family and continue to extend outwards. Most importantly consider friends of friends: these are your acquaintances. Research findings consistently point to the value of remote associations in networking. These distant well-wishers have proved to be more likely to make referrals.

While you are deciding on members of your network, think about what they might add to it. Are they going to help you? Or can you help them in some way? You could divide up the starting point for your network by categorizing people by your professional assets.

What are professional assets?

They are your education and skills, your character (in particular your ability to interact, negotiate, persuade and influence), and your experience and past achievements. To begin with, everyone in your network will share a commonality with at least one of your professional assets.

Effective networking comes into its own when you are embarking on a new career or hobby or interest. This is when you need to extend the reach of your network and draw upon strangers' knowledge. Eventually the most powerful professional asset that you will have will be your network.

What makes a good network?

A good network is typified by a high number of distant well-wishers and frequent use. Diversity is crucial too, because it generates a larger network with a greater information flow.

What's the best way to network?

You need to get out there and meet your network, stay in touch and keep the lines of communication open.

How do you overcome shyness?

Everybody is apprehensive about meeting new people. Focus on establishing relationships rather than winning the 'salesperson of the year golden globe award'. Ask lots of questions, but make sure that you listen to the answers. Know how to describe what you do in a way that defines the benefit to your customers. Also know who your typical customers are, so that you can get the most out of networking.

What's the best way to start a conversation?

You could start a conversation by saying something like, 'Hello, I'm so-and-so. What do you do?' If you have to break into a group, just ask 'Do you mind if I join you?' and be assumptive. No one's going to say 'No'.

What's the best way to end a conversation?

Summarize what was discussed, and if it's appropriate to talk about a follow-up lunch or meeting then do so.

What impact does networking have on an individual's career?

It increases your choices because it is likely to lead to a referral from another. It helps you tap into the hidden jobs market – that is, jobs that are not advertised. It ensures that you keep up to date with changes. And it means that you have access to an ever-widening pool of expert advice. All this goes a long way towards empowering you, either in your current role or in a new one.

Networking summary

To sum up, a good network, one that is large and diverse, can create career opportunities and empower the individual. Building a powerful network is a long process, so to expedite network growth you should develop your network around your professional assets, and seize networking opportunities. For detailed dos and don'ts see the list below. If you would like to learn more about networking, see Appendix 1 for details of the Powermingle site and networking books, with reviews for each.

In networking, do:

- [ ] be bold;
- [ ] invest time in building your network;
- [ ] identify professional organizations or events that can help to build your network;
- [ ] develop your network around your professional assets;
- [ ] relationship build;
- [ ] identify your ideal customer;
- [ ] know how you can benefit a customer or associate;
- [ ] keep your network up to date;
- [ ] focus on building 'far' relationships;
- [ ] listen and follow up where appropriate.

And don't:

- [ ] be shy;
- [ ] expect a quick win;
- [ ] self-promote to people who already think you're wonderful, like your Mum;
- [ ] grow your network around one single achievement;
- [ ] sell;
- [ ] be unclear who your prospects are;
- [ ] be vague about what you have to offer;
- [ ] use your business cards as coasters;
- [ ] focus on developing 'close' relationships into friendships;
- [ ] procrastinate over networking opportunities.

Networking can be put to use to great effect when job seeking. In Chapter 2 our example parent used networking to increase her knowledge of the role of teaching and to build a client list. When you are trying to access the hidden jobs, market networking can enable job-seeking success.

THE HIDDEN JOBS MARKET

Ask an expert

Neil Lewis is the Managing Director of career management providers Working Careers, a wholly owned subsidiary of Fairplace plc. Neil has over

15 years of personal development experience. It was his desire to empower the individual to manage their own career effectively that created the impetus for Working Careers, which Neil co-founded in 1993. Working Careers delivers career coaching, interview technique training and CV writing services to job seekers (http://www.workthingcareers.com). Fairplace plc provides outplacement solutions to businesses during major transitional stages such as mergers and acquisitions, downsizing implementation and HR restructuring (http://www.fairplace.com).

What is the 'hidden jobs market'?

The hidden jobs market is every job that is never advertised externally. It is made up of: all internal listed vacancies, jobs that are filled through speculative applications, jobs that are outsourced to headhunters (executive search agencies) and jobs that are filled via an existing employee's referral.

Why does the hidden jobs market make up two-thirds of the total jobs market?

I know it's an astonishingly high figure. However, if we look at those employers that do advertise externally, they tend to be high volume recruiters and public sector organizations. They advertise because they have a recruitment demand to fulfil and they have the budgets to support the cost of advertising. But 60 per cent of companies in the UK are SMEs (small to medium sized enterprises), and they are not high volume recruiters. In addition the cost of advertising is often prohibitive for them. Also, unlike higher volume recruiters, they rarely have an HR department or even an HR person. If this is the case it means that they do not have anybody to manage recruitment, or for that matter personal development.

When we run workshops and we ask candidates how they got their current job, most will say that they got it through referral. For example a friend or business associate may have seen a position become vacant and put forward the candidate's name. Referral or networking is a low cost, low risk way for companies and organizations to recruit. Some even offer employee reward schemes for every successful referral.

Others say they got their job by applying speculatively: that is, offering their services to a company when the company is looking to recruit for the same position. Or they have previously speculatively applied to a company that subsequently contacts the candidate when a suitable position arises.

Some say that they found their job through a recruitment consultant or headhunter. By far the fewest say they found their job as a result of responding to an advertisement.

How do candidates go about uncovering hidden jobs?

They have to be proactive and it's very hard work. It is completely different from responding to an advertisement, which is reactive. They have to approach their job search as a politician would campaign management. Primarily they need to understand that all recruitment is a function of economics. It's all about supply and demand. So, to uncover the hidden jobs market a candidate should be looking for where the demand is in the marketplace. Who needs their skills and expertise? How can they solve their prospective employer's business problem?

Once a candidate has discovered a gap in the market, where demand exists, he or she should set about matching it to his or her work preferences. The opportunity needs to be in the right location, carry an appropriate remuneration package, deliver personal development opportunities and so on.

The next step is to build a database of companies and organizations that might require his or her services. Candidates need to include the name of the person that would be their prospective boss in the database. They can then start to send out speculative applications. They could employ the 'blunderbuss' approach and send their CV to everybody, but this is largely ineffective. We recommend a targeted approach.

What's the split between chance and preparation or research in finding hidden jobs?

It's probably about nine to one in favour of preparation and research. We advise candidates to send an intelligently targeted cover letter and CV to their prospective boss, and then follow up with a phone call to the recipient. In our experience if they apply in this way, then they will be hired if there is a suitable position available. Why wouldn't the company or organization fill the position at no cost and minimum effort to them?

If the position that is sought is not available at the time of applying, then that's when the element of chance gains momentum. Unless the candidate continues to make follow-up calls, he or she may miss out on the opportunity when the position becomes free. He or she might lose the position to a referral or another speculative applicant who is fresher in their prospective boss's mind. So the timing of the application is where chance plays a greater role. But if the application is inappropriate – that is, not researched – then chance plays no part in the appointment. See Appendix 3 for how to make speculative applications.

So if a candidate is speculating or networking, how does he or she convince a prospective employer that it should hire him or her?

Whether speculating or networking, candidates need a story for their skills or expertise. They should consider themselves as sole traders, where they are the product. They have to know their USP (unique selling proposition), what differentiates them from others, how they can benefit their prospective employer. To quote President Kennedy, 'Ask not what your country can do for you – ask what you can do for your country.' They need to view themselves through their prospective employer's eyes. They need to know the answer to the recruiter's question, 'What can you do for me?'

Networking when job seeking is essentially a verbal form of speculatively applying for jobs. High volume is an important function of both networking and speculative application success. The better the network, the wider and larger it is. The more speculative applications a candidate makes, the greater the probability of securing a new job.

Networking also serves two other job seeking purposes. If candidates are struggling to find their gap in a market, they should call people in their target companies or organizations and ask them about their industry. Books, trade publications and even Web sites can be out of date, so it's important that candidates check their information. Unless the candidate knows who his or her prospective boss would be, he or she should again call the target company and ask. There is no point in sending a carefully researched cover letter and CV to the wrong person.

With unemployment at such a low rate, do the job hunting techniques that you have talked about still work in a tight market?

Yes. There is still as much churn (employees leaving companies) as there always was. This means that opportunities still exist in companies, because there is a natural wastage of staff. People retire, take career breaks, get promoted, leave and work for someone else, or change from full time to part time work.

There is also a shortage of skilled labour. Two to three years ago IT skills were in great demand, now there is a shortage of trade skills such as: plumbing, carpentry and bricklaying. So there is now a gap in the market for tradespeople.

Some careers authors advise candidates to pitch their prospective employers for jobs. First, would you also recommend this?

If a candidate has the confidence and has done the research, then yes, I would recommend this. I wouldn't advise a candidate to do it totally cold, without doing any research, or if he or she didn't feel sure of the approach.

If a candidate chooses to pitch a prospective employer, he or she needs to consider the timing of their call. He or she might annoy the prospective boss by calling him or her at a bad time. Psychologically people are more receptive to calls mid-week when they've got over Monday and are starting to look forward to the weekend. A prospective boss may have more time to speak outside of office hours. Anyone making such a call will face the usual obstacles of protective secretaries and receptionists who want to minimize any disruption to their boss's schedule.

Second, how should a candidate go about it?

Our preferred approach is that candidates send an intelligent targeted cover letter and CV first, and then follow up with a call. Most candidates are operating a little outside of their comfort zone when they make a follow-up call. This is eased if a candidate can talk to his or her prospective boss about the cover letter and CV.

As proactive job seeking is a full-time job, we recommend that candidates treat their job search as they would going to work. They should create a space in their home, dress as if for work and plan their speculative applications as they would a working day. We estimate that a targeted cover letter and appropriate CV take between two hours and half a day to write. It is time consuming because of the research, preparation and networking that ensures a targeted result. The cover letter and CV should demonstrate to the prospective employer how the candidate could benefit him or her and the organization.

The starting point for any candidate's job search is to identify his or her 'zone of possibility' (see Figure 9.1). This represents the jobs that the candidate believes he or she can do. The more progressive the career move, the higher the amount of effort that is required for the job search. These high aspirational jobs are housed in the first priority zone: zone A. Zone B houses job opportunities that are on the same level with the candidate's existing or last job. These career moves are usually lateral ones. If a candidate becomes dispirited, perhaps because he or she has been made redundant or has been job seeking without success for a long time, he or she may start to talk about settling for any job. These types of jobs are housed in the last zone: zone C. Candidates expect to be able to attain these jobs easily, as they are lesser roles than the candidate has previously fulfilled. The danger with this is that candidates focus their effort on zone C jobs, when they should be focusing their effort on zone A jobs.

In addition, candidates wrongly believe that companies will place them in zone C jobs. Prospective employers don't want to hire a former general manager to stack shelves! There is an obvious mismatch with the candidate and the job, which points to the general manager leaving as soon as a better offer comes along. So we recommend that candidates identify jobs that fall within zone A, and channel their job seeking efforts into applying for these roles. When referring to the hidden jobs market, we advise candidates to use the targeted speculative application approach, and register with headhunter recruitment consultancies where appropriate.

Hidden jobs market summary

Creative job hunting involves identifying where a demand exists, and meeting it. Typically the demand will not be advertised, so the right person for the job needs to advertise him or herself to prospective employers. Traditional advertising usually builds brand awareness and sometimes leads to a purchase. Speculative applications have much the same effect. They increase for many prospective employers the realization of how the candidate might benefit the organization. For some prospective employers the candidate will call or apply at a time when there is a suitable position to be filled, the advertising equivalent of a purchase. Here is a summary of tips on how to access the hidden jobs market.

Do:

- [ ] research companies to see if there is a demand for your services;
- [ ] check your information by calling the prospective organization;
- [ ] treat your speculative applications like going to work;
- [ ] build up a database of prospective employers and their organizations;
- [ ] send intelligent targeted applications where the benefit to the organization is clear;
- [ ] follow up a mailout with a phone call;

☐ go after zone A jobs;
☐ know your employability-worth.

Don't:

☐ treat your CV as if it's a chain letter;
☐ rely on indifferent information;
☐ busy yourself with nagging little DIY chores instead;
☐ forget to log the applications and calls that you have made;
☐ send a CV about what you want out of your next career move;
☐ assume that your CV and covering letter will be filed in the right place;
☐ go after zone C jobs;
☐ associate rejection with inability: 'recruitment is a function of economics'.

HEADHUNTERS

As with other job-hunting techniques, your headhunter or recruitment consultancy needs to be appropriate to the type of job seeker that you are, and specialize in your career of choice. In general headhunters find you, and you find recruitment consultancies. Headhunters' area of expertise lies in their ability to fill challenging vacancies. The position to be filled might be a sensitive one that cannot be advertised: for example an organization may be looking to replace a senior manager, and may not wish to alert its competitors or its own staff to the forthcoming change. Or an organization may need to recruit an executive to spearhead a new project, which means that it may be recruiting outside its core business function.

As a general rule, headhunter vacancies are not advertised externally. Headhunters specialize in knowing who's who in a given sector, and how they can be contacted discreetly. Usually they work on specific assignments for employers, and approach prospective candidates. It used to be the case that candidates were advised against contacting headhunters directly. With the advent of the Internet, some headhunters and executive search and selection consultancies encourage candidates to upload their CVs onto their candidate databases. If you upload your CV onto a headhunter or search and selection database, you should expect to receive some form of confirmation of receipt from the consultancy.

Executive selection consultancies sit between headhunters and recruitment consultancies. They generally both advertise executive positions to be filled, and retain a database of suitable candidates. If you want an executive selection consultancy to keep a record of your CV, you should e-mail them a copy. If the consultancy has its own online CV pro forma, you should complete it. It is far easier for consultancies to manage data if it is stored electronically, and you are more likely to be contacted if you have sent your CV in an electronic format, because electronic data can be retrieved at any time and does not rely on human memory.

Headhunting and executive search have long been the preserve of specialists who were unwilling to share trade secrets with non-execs. As a consequence very little is known about headhunting. As headhunters are widely renowned for their superior hunting techniques, we wanted to see what lessons could be learnt from an expert.

Ask a headhunter

Graham Roadnight is the Managing Director of Drax, a pan-European executive search firm that headhunts talent for senior management and board-level roles (http://www.draxexecutive.com). Drax was created in October 2000, following one of the fastest recorded management buyouts from the world's third largest recruitment group, and owners of the seventh largest executive search firm, Spherion. Its execution of its own MBO reflects the aggression to achieve against tight timelines that is reflected today in its client-mandated work.

Drax provides senior mangers to clients from high technology and communications, media and entertainment, public affairs and corporate communications, venture capital and financial services, the public sector and utilities, as well as a specialist diversity and corporate social responsibility practice.

Can you give an example of a recent assignment that Drax fulfilled?

In March 2003 we were awarded a mandate to source a shortlist of finance directors for the plc board of a FTSE 250 leading service provider.

The salary was set in a range from £200,000 to £250,000. We were working to a tight deadline because the client required delivery of the shortlist on the twentieth day from commencement of the assignment.

Our client had already awarded the mandate to a different company, but was disillusioned as five months had passed and it had still not received an acceptable shortlist. It required a finance director who possessed strong relationships with the analyst community. The new finance director needed to possess an unblemished track record, and to have demonstrated a personal impact on the organizations he or she had represented. Due to external dynamics, if we did not present the shortlist within 20 working days the role would be placed on hold, and our client could be susceptible to an aggressive takeover.

Having received a full client briefing, which included the required skills, experience and credibility of the candidate sought, we then explored the business objectives that needed to be captured from this new hire. During the exploration phase of the briefing we were able to suggest a number of areas that were not originally considered. We were able to achieve this through leveraging off both our industry insight and experience, and in so doing provided additional value.

We accepted the mandate and we delivered the shortlist on the tenth day. All candidates on our shortlist were cross-referenced with the analyst community, and we were confident that they could achieve the objective that they were being hired for. Such was our confidence that we agreed to defer part of our final payment for a period of six months, to provide our client with the opportunity to feel the impact of its new finance director.

How is speed a measure of success in headhunting?

In our experience we have found the contrary to be true: there exists an inverted snobbery attached to speed in the search and selection industry. This is almost to the point that the longer the search takes, the higher inference there is to quality. Conversely the sooner the shortlist is delivered, the higher the inference is that quality has been compromised.

Speed, if not always a benefit when delivering a mandate as exampled above, is a direct reflection of the extent of market knowledge and network that the search firm possesses. The difference between a 12-week and a four-week shortlist delivery time is knowledge.

At Drax we invest heavily in continual development of market knowledge. We believe that our clients retain us to leverage off our market knowledge and achieve the highest results. We do not believe that the retained fee paid by our clients is designed to fund our businesses research of client markets.

How do headhunter and executive search assignments differ from those of a recruitment consultancy?

Invariably the assignments that we manage are for jobs that are not advertised. Clients generally retain executive search firms as they wish to leverage off the firm's market knowledge and executive network. Executive search is commonly client-centric.

Clients generally undergo a careful due diligence process to ensure that they are awarding their mandate to the best firm who can execute it successfully. Equally for every new mandate received, the search firm will develop an individual interpretation of the client's strategic hiring policy. The firm would then typically build a specific proposal illustrating exactly what it would undertake to achieve success. It is this pre-engagement phase that creates a considered and controlled search, thus producing for both the client and customer a service designed to deliver qualitative results.

Executive search firms trade off their intellectual capital or informed market intelligence (IMI), and provide their professional resources of time and material to create a solution that fits exactly the client's needs. The service is a tailored one designed to produce a bespoke result. Executive search firms usually possess a deep understanding of either an industry sector or a discipline or specialist area of expertise. In many cases industry knowledge and discipline expertise are interdependent, and so the firm has a sophisticated understanding of both. At Drax we have an Intelligence Unit that specializes in developing IMI and contacts with thought leaders in our sectors.

How has the Internet impacted search and selection?

Though the process for gaining an assignment remains the same, in that it is client-led, the way that candidates network and garner knowledge and information has changed. On the Drax site (http://www. draxexecutive.com), for example, candidates can search on location and role to view recent assignments. They can also research us, which has impacted the transparency of what search and selection firms do. Candidates may also post an electronic copy of their CV to us.

Whereas, in the past, candidates were advised against contacting search and selection firms, this is now something that is acceptable. Firms are only able to consider candidates for a role in the unlikely event that a suitable current assignment exists. Drax works with select individuals to provide a career coaching function, and also work with third party business psychologists. We also provide other value added services such as access to networking events, industry forums and market intelligence.

What challenges does the search and selection industry face?

The executive search industry will have to evolve in order to survive. Many of the larger search firms have stood still for 30 years, relying on the 'old boys' network' and actively resisting change. Drax are committed to change and to creating new solutions that are in tune with market demand.

We have a responsibility to provide our clients with the best talent, to ensure a robust future economy in the UK. This is the nucleus of the 'cradle to grave' philosophy, one that supports the thesis that today's student part-timer may be tomorrow's chief executive. This objective is supported through ensuring that we have a successive supply of high calibre senior managers. Though today's graduates are not the type of candidates that we would headhunt, in 10 or 15 years' time they could be. We work closely with business schools and universities such as Oxford and Cambridge to develop career planning ideas for tomorrow's leaders.

Drax is also a Human Capital Partner to Business in the Community, which is the influential thought leader on corporate sustainability amongst the FTSE 100, and a division of the Prince's Trust.

As technology advances and the use of artificial intelligence (AI) and broadband spreads, we should expect to see search and selection utilizing these developments to expedite assignments. It is unlikely that the human element will be replaced, but technological advances serve to complement it in fulfilling clients' mandates.

We are currently in a knowledge-sharing information age. Search firms can embrace this by continuing to increase their transparency with both clients and candidates. Most search firms produce a regular flow of published white papers, industry reviews and market analysis, and stage key industry events. This approach is likely to encourage repeat business from clients and superior senior managers. We have developed a quarterly industry review (see http://whistleblower. draxexecutive.com) as a forum for knowledge sharing.

RECRUITMENT CONSULTANCIES

Recruitment consultancies are professional employment agencies. Companies and organizations use recruitment consultancies to fill vacancies with quality candidates quickly. Ordinarily an employer will advertise for candidates as well as using a recruitment consultancy. Recruitment consultancies usually require candidates to complete a CV, electronic or otherwise. Headhunters, executive search agencies and recruitment consultancies all generate income by placing suitable candidates in suitable jobs.

As a result, recruitment consultants and headhunters rely on their ability to source the right candidate for a job to earn their fees. When deliberating with a recruitment consultant or headhunter, be sure to make them fully aware of your employability worth. Most will be happy to help you convince prospective employers that you are a hugely valuable resource.

Ask a recruitment consultant

Janet McGlaughlin is the Operations Director for Pertemps Recruitment Partner (http://www.pertemps.co.uk). We asked her to share her thoughts on choosing a recruitment consultancy with us.

What advice would you give to candidates when selecting a recruitment consultancy?

When candidates select a recruitment consultancy their goal should be to choose the consultancy that is the most likely to find them a suitable job. Candidates should be confident that the agency they select will do this for them should a suitable job opportunity arise. We would recommend the following:

- [ ] Research the recruitment consultancy via its Web site before visiting it.
- [ ] If you have a niche specialism, choose a sector specialist recruitment consultancy.
- [ ] Check for professional memberships such as the Recruitment and Employment Confederation and the Confederation of British Industry.

When a candidate goes to an agency in the street, he or she should check that the consultant:

- [ ] Gives them a meaningful interview which explores every aspect of their employment history. Be prepared to be assessed.
- [ ] Has a good level of industry knowledge.
- [ ] Is prepared to consider him or her for roles which may not match his or her actual work experience. The consultant should match

transferable skills and work preferences to suitable roles. We train our consultants to avoid thinking, 'a round peg must go in a round hole'.

Candidates should remember that consultants try to match candidates to the most suitable job opportunities, so the best agency is not necessarily the one that offers a candidate a job the soonest. The size of the agency is not as important as the first impression that a candidate gets from a consultant. We would advise candidates to research the agency but to also follow their instincts.

Recruit zone A consultants

If your profession is outside of the scope of a particular recruitment consultancy, then ask the consultant if he or she can recommend an agency that better meets your requirements. To maximize your job search you should sign up with appropriate recruitment consultancies, that is those that fall within zones A and B of your zones of possibility job choices. Remember, as a suitable candidate you have the potential to increase an agency's income. Appendix 2 has details on specific recruitment consultancies by industry sector and job seeker type.

ADVERTISED JOBS

Given that few jobs are advertised externally you should endeavour to have sight of all jobs that are relevant to your job search. As with job market research, there are two main ways to view advertisements: online and in print. Regardless of the medium you use to view advertised jobs, the principles behind finding suitable vacancies are similar.

Print advertisements

Advertised jobs can be found in both the trade press (by industry sector categorization) and national and regional newspapers, by industry sector categorization and locality categorization respectively. Often occupational vacancy listings are advertised on specific days.

If you are job seeking you should ensure that you get every publication that carries relevant vacancies. If you buy a regional newspaper you may have to search through the vacancy listings for your relevant occupations. The trade press and national papers (on certain days) tend to be industry specific. Keep a record of every advertisement that you respond to, much like the speculative job application log.

When responding to advertisements send an appropriate cover letter and CV. (There are examples of CVs and cover letter formats in Chapters 5 and 6.) It is advisable to send an electronic version of your CV and cover letter in response to an advertisement. In a recent survey conducted by reed.co.uk, '78 per cent of recruiters said that if they had to choose between two equal candidates, one with a paper CV and one with an electronic CV, they would pick the electronic CV first every time' (http://www.therecruitmentconsultant.co.uk, January 2003).

The exception to this is when the recruiter specifically asks for a paper version of a CV. The format in which a recruiter can read a CV in is determined by the human resource management (HRM) system he or she uses. Some recruiters have fully automated systems. These recruiters can search CVs electronically, in much the same way as an Internet keyword search. Recruiters who do not have automated HRM systems cannot search for or read electronic CVs. They can only read electronic CVs if they print them out, which involves extra work for them. That is why it is important to comply with advertisers' wishes about your CV format. (See Chapter 6 for CV tips.)

Online advertisements

Online advertisements can be found on:

- [ ] job boards;
- [ ] search and selection and recruitment consultancies' sites;
- [ ] corporate sites: look for links to 'employment opportunities', 'recruitment', 'working for {companyname}' on these sites;
- [ ] some portals such as http://www.yell.com, http://www.yahoo.com, and http://www.handbag.com.

If you do not know the URLs of sites that carry advertisements to match your job searches, you can use Internet search engines to find them (for a list see Appendix 1). Your job search should include words like: 'marketing jobs UK'.

In general, job boards carry the greatest number of online advertisements, so you should start your job search here. Here are some UK job boards:

Workthing: www.workthing.com

This site carries award winning careers editorial content and job search functionality. Features include interviews with industry experts, lowdowns, professional career management services, a national salary checker, online employment law advice, and the ability to search by company name. Candidates can register for e-mail job alerts and register to receive work-related newsletters.

PeopleBank: www.peoplebank.com

The PeopleBank site was one of the first CV databases in the UK. Candidates can search for a job, register for e-mail job alerts, complete an online CV, and register to receive newsletters. Recruiters subscribe to search the CV database, and contact candidates by e-mail.

Fish4: www.fish4.co.uk

Candidates can search for a job, car or home on this site. Fish4's affiliation with the *Manchester Evening News* makes this site a great source for jobs in the northwest of England.

If you do search for a job via a job board you should do the following:

- ☐ Set up an e-mail job alert.
- ☐ Complete an online CV.
- ☐ Register for newsletters: these will contain job seeking tips and may be sponsored by recruiters.

SET UP E-MAIL JOB ALERTS

If you visit a job board site and search for a job you will be asked to fill in certain search criteria. The usual criteria are type of job, occupation, location and in some cases salary. Once you submit your job search, the engine searches all published vacancies for those that match your criteria. By setting up an e-mail job alert you are effectively saving a job search to match against future published advertisements. So if you set up a job alert you will be e-mailed with a list of every newly published vacancy that matches your job alert criteria.

Job alert systems usually search across the following content in a published vacancy:

- [ ] job title;
- [ ] a proportion of the job description text;
- [ ] location;
- [ ] on occasion, salary or company name.

To ensure that you find every appropriate job advertisement, you should do the following:

- [ ] Make sure your e-mail address is correct. The job board will not be able to e-mail you if it is incorrect.
- [ ] When selecting your occupation group, save all possible job title combinations. For example you might check 'retail manager', 'sales manager', 'account manager', 'store manager' and 'buyer'.
- [ ] Keep the location categorization broad, for example the southeast as opposed to London, since location category catchment areas vary from site to site.
- [ ] Do not include salary. Many recruiters do not put salary details in job advertisements, which means that relevant advertisements may not be found.
- [ ] Set up e-mail job alerts on every appropriate site.

REGISTER YOUR CV ONLINE

In addition to setting up job alerts you should register your CV with job boards that have CV database functionality. In general recruiters pay to search a CV database for a set period of time. CV database search results are rendered by relevance to CV matching search criteria (for example, 'three years' retail management experience') *if* the CV has been recently updated. Most CV databases will not include old CVs in the recruiter's search results. CV cut-off periods can vary from one to six months depending on the job board. The most recently updated CV that matches the employer's requirements will be shown first in the recruiter's search results. This means that your CV may not be found unless you update it regularly (at least once a month). The impetus for this is that recruiters want to be able to rely on the information that is held in your CV, the assumption being that the more recent the information, the more accurate it is.

If you are applying for jobs via a corporate site you will need to supply your CV in the organization's desired format. Some corporate sites have a job search function, and provide online CV pro formas or online application forms. If there are no vacancies matching your job search on a corporate site, you should still fill out the company's online CV pro forma, if it has one. This is the equivalent to an electronic speculative application. As such, you should follow up on an electronic CV submission with a phone call to your prospective boss. If the corporate site does not have a job search or online CV function, you should treat the site as part research for your speculative applications. You could either e-mail or post your CV and cover letter to your prospective employer, depending on the format the organization prefers.

As with print advertisement responses, you should keep a tally of all the online applications you make. Examples of cover letters and CVs in various formats are in Chapters 5 and 6 respectively.

For the best job hunting results it is advisable to vary your hunting style. Concentrate on zone A jobs and uncovering the hidden jobs market. Sign up to any relevant search and selection or recruitment consultancies that can bring jobs to you. Set up e-mail alerts and register your CV online so that recruiters can find you. For the best results start your campaign early. Securing a new job can take from three to six months upwards. If you get tired of the chase, remember that for the right employer you are a hugely valuable resource.

RECRUITMENT AND JOB FAIRS

Recruitment fairs are generally advertised in the local press, or occasionally on online job boards. The prospective employers that exhibit at recruitment fairs normally hope to fill a high volume of vacancies. If you attend a job fair you will usually be competing with a large number of similarly skilled or experienced candidates, so in order to stand out from the competition you should prepare for a recruitment fair as if you were going for an interview with every company that you are interested in. If the recruitment fair advertisement is online you should be able to link to company information. If the fair is not advertised online, you could call the venue and ask to be sent a list of exhibitors. Ask for the exhibitors' list in an online format, if available. This will save you valuable research time as you should be able to link to company information from the list. If the information is scant, go beyond it and utilize the company research tips from Chapter 3.

Prepare a list of questions for your prospective employers, and dress as you would for an interview. Take enough copies of your CV for each prospective employer, and aim to collect business cards from every recruiter that you speak to. Some recruiters interview at recruitment fairs, some ask candidates to complete screening tests or questionnaires. If you expect this to happen, you should perform better than those candidates that have not prepared as thoroughly.

Now that you are well versed in job tracking tactics, the next task is to develop your job catching skills. As second chances to catch jobs are rarer than thought-leading sound bites from David Brent, getting it right the first time is fundamental to job hunting success. In the next chapter we will discover how to create lasting first impressions that leave the recruiter with a desire to know more.

5 Make the right first impression

A first impression is the first communication that a prospective employee makes with his or her prospective employer. Whether the first communication is spoken or written, it should achieve two aims. We can liken the aims to the purposes of product packaging, which attract the consumer's attention and describe the benefits of the contents in a simple, enticing fashion.

A cover letter or first conversation is CV packaging. It should attract the recruiter's attention by answering the recruiter's question, 'How can you help my organization?' It should concisely describe the benefits that the candidate could bring to the organization, as a prelude to the complete explanation contained in the CV.

One way to decide what to highlight in a cover letter is to take what recruiters ask for in job advertisements and detail that in the letter. What recruiters want can be termed 'employer's requirements'. They are usually featured in the main body of the job advertisement. The employer's requirements are normally expressed as minimums of either:

- [ ] qualifications;
- [ ] skills;
- [ ] experience;
- [ ] a combination of the above.

Examples of two vacancies are detailed in the boxes.

Example 1: field social worker vacancy advertised on Workthing.com

Description: Company A is a rapidly expanding independent sector organization providing services to help communities cope

---

with the use of illicit drugs. Company A's Young People's Drug Service is an exciting new project in Sheffield aiming to provide advice, information and support around drug issues and, where appropriate, supporting young people into treatment.

You will need an understanding of drug-related issues and how these impact on young people, and ideally you should have a track record of working with young people in a one-to-one or group work setting.

For an informal discussion on this post please contact Sam Smith, Director of Operations–Community Services, on 12345 678910.

Company A cannot confirm any appointment until a Criminal Records Bureau check is satisfactorily completed.

You will need to have a relevant professional qualification or at least two years' experience in the field.

Example 2: sales manager vacancy advertised on Workthing.com

Job purpose: To manage a number of small direct sales teams ensuring targets are achieved on a daily basis in line with the organization's targets set. Obtaining personal injury claims for referral to specialist solicitors by managing the canvassing teams under your control. Leading the teams by daily support and coaching through effective and excellent communication.

Remuneration: In line with all our direct sales positions this role is an employed position with all the benefits offered within the group. A basic salary of £21,000.00 with OTE of £42,000.00 (no upper limit). Executive fully expensed car. Pension after qualifying period, to which the company contributes 3%. 22 days' holiday per year plus all UK bank holidays.

Skills/knowledge/experience:
☐   A proven ability in successfully leading sales teams in a competitive environment.

☐ Excellent communication skills.
☐ Able to demonstrate successful leadership through development and support of others.
☐ Full UK driving licence.
☐ Performance driven individual motivated to succeed.

Location: North West Region.

Send your CV and covering letter to the Group HR Manager. Click here to apply online.

FIT TO EMPLOYER REQUIREMENTS

A cover letter should be structured around the employer's requirements as featured in an advertisement. Most job descriptions consist of a trade-off between skills, qualifications and experience, as you can see from Example 1, where Company A requires either a 'professional qualification' or 'at least two years' relevant experience'. These are minimum requirements as far as the prospective employer is concerned. It is good practice to highlight the employer's requirements in a job advertisement so that you do not miss any key points in your cover letter. For an example of highlighted employer's requirements for the field social worker vacancy see Figure 5.1, where they are circled and linked to the appropriate descriptions.

You should compare the employer's requirements with your abilities, and see how well they match. The better they match, the happier you should be fulfilling the role. It may help you to compare your abilities to the employer's requirements if you rank their match in order of priority for the employer, perhaps with 1 equals low and 4 equals high (see Table 5.1 for an example).

Description:

Company A is a rapidly expanding independent sector organi[**Communication & counselling skills**]
services to help communities cope with the use of illicit drugs

Company A's Young People's Drug Service is an exciting new project in
Sheffield aiming to provide advice, information and support around drug issues
and, where appropriate, supporting young people into treatment.

You will need an understanding of drug-related issues and how these impact on
young people, and ideally you should have a track record of working with
young people in a one-to-one or group work setting.

For an informal discussion on this post please contact Sam Smith, Director of
Operations—Community Services, on 12345 678910.

Company A cannot confirm any appointment until a Criminal Records Bureau
check is satisfactorily completed.

You will need to have a relevant professional qualification or at least two years'
experience in the field.

Figure 5.1 *Field social worker advertisement with employer's requirements circled*

Table 5.1   *Employer's requirements ranked*

Skills	**Employer's priority rank**	**Qualifications**	**Rank**	**Experience**	**Rank**
Communication Advice and information One to one and group settings with young people	3	*Understanding* of drug-related issues	3	*Track record* of working with young people/one to one and group settings	4
Counselling Support around drug issues	3	Relevant *professional qualification*	4 **OR**	*two years'* *experience* in the field	4

COVER LETTERS

A cover letter in response to the field social worker vacancy might look like the example in the box.

Example cover letter response to advertisement

Sam Smith
Operations Director
Community Services
Company A
Sheffield
SG1 3GH

Flat 4 Orchard Court
London Road
Sheffield
SG4 7UT

Vacancy reference: WT/786

5th January 2003

Dear Ms Smith,
I am writing in response to your advertisement for the position of a field social worker.

Please find attached my CV detailing over three years' field social work experience. Much of my casework was with young people. In particular:

☐ I can demonstrate that through my work on family drug rehabilitation programmes I was able to reduce instances of violence through increased understanding of addiction.

☐ Where appropriate I was able to support individuals into treatment.

Your plans for rapid expansion seem very exciting to me. I would welcome the opportunity of discussing how I can add value to your team with you.

I look forward to hearing from you.

Yours sincerely,
Chris Brewster.
(Content provided courtesy of Working Careers)

The applicant matches his abilities to the employer's requirements and comments on his work preference. He alludes to his preference for a 'rapidly expanding' organization. It is good practice to use the same phraseology as is displayed in the advertisement, as in 'rapidly expanding'. This should create a feeling of symmetry between the applicant and the recruiter. These general principles can be applied to all cover letter writing. Unless the prospective employer has specifically requested otherwise, you should send a cover letter with every application that you make (including electronic ones). Examples of speculative application and headhunter cover letters are given in the boxes.

Suggested alternative opening lines for speculative cover letters

I read with interest the *Yorkshire Herald* report that your company is planning to open a new office in this area, and therefore ...

Following the appointment of your new Chairperson and the proposed changes in your organization ...

Having recently read your case study outlining the launch of your new widget ...

Following a conversation with ...

(Content provided courtesy of Working Careers)

Example of a speculative cover letter

Mr Philip Steadman
Operations Director
Fast Delivery
20 High Street
Linktown
Kent TN13 9BN

47 Chaucer Lane
Stonebury
SB21 4AP

01234 567891

5th January 2003

Dear Mr Steadman,

Your company has established a reputation over the past few years for professionalism and consistent growth, and recent publicity in the press suggests that you have ambitious plans.

I am an experienced warehouse manager looking to develop my career within the consumer products area. As you will see from my enclosed CV I have expertise in:

- ☐ managing all aspects of warehouse distribution
- ☐ introducing quality control systems into labour intensive environments
- ☐ computerized supply chain management and computer aided design systems.

I would welcome the opportunity to discuss any areas of interest within Fast Delivery, and if I may, I will contact you over the coming week to arrange a mutually agreed appointment time.

Yours sincerely,
Lesley Jones.
(Content provided courtesy of Working Careers)

Example of a cover letter for headhunter search and selection consultancy

Consultant's name   Your address
Position/job title
Agency name
Agency address

5th January 2003

Dear Name,

Following my recent call to your office, I have enclosed my CV as requested. You will see that I am an experienced middle office manager with a proven track record of implementing strategic systems in major banking operation.

I have been exposed to many functions of banking throughout my career, predominantly:

- [ ] heading a professional team – recruiting, training and motivating personnel at all levels
- [ ] facilitating close liaison and effective communications between departments
- [ ] inputting new systems in conjunction with IT
- [ ] working within set timeframes to restricted budgets.

I am now seeking to further my career utilizing the wealth of experience gained in middle office management, and would therefore welcome the opportunity to discuss any future opportunities suitable to my experience.

Should my CV prove of interest to you, or if you would like further information from me, please do not hesitate to contact me on: 09876 543210.

I look forward to hearing from you.

Yours sincerely,
Jo Malik.
(Content provided courtesy of Working Careers)

As a former executive search consultant, Martin John Yate (author of *Great Answers to Tough Interview Questions*, 2001) developed the executive briefing cover letter. The purpose of the executive briefing is to explain quickly to the recruiter why the candidate fits the role. It can negate the need to alter your CV, as the executive briefing highlights the relevant parts of your CV. This approach is also helpful if your application is going to a large organization, where several people may be involved in the hiring process. It does not matter whether or not the person who reads your cover letter is an expert in your field. He or she should understand how suitable you are from the executive briefing. If you use the executive briefing you can tell the recruiter precisely how well your credentials match the requirements, which will save him or her time. For an example of the executive briefing see the box.

Example of an executive briefing

Dear Sir/Madam (if name not known),
While my attached CV will provide you with a general outline of my work history, my problem solving abilities, and some achievements, I have taken the time to list your current specific requirements and my applicable skills in those areas. I hope that this will enable you to use your time effectively today.

Your requirements:	My skills:
1. Management of public library service area (for circulation, reference, etc.)	1. Experience as head reference librarian at University of Smithtown
2. Supervision of 14 full-time support employees	2. Supervised support staff of 17
3. Ability to work with larger supervisory team in planning, budgeting and policy formulating	3. Responsible for budget and reformation of circulation rules during my last year
4. ALA	4. I have this qualification
5. Three years' experience	5. One year with public library, two with University of Smithtown

(Source: Yate, 2001)

E-mail cover letters

You should e-mail a cover letter if the recruiter specifically requests one, or if there is no mention of a cover letter in the job advertisement. This is advisable for two reasons. First, if the recruiter is unable to open your CV attachment he or she will still know enough about you to be able to make a decision about shortlisting you. Second, if your CV is not specifically targeted to the job, you can highlight the relevant parts of your CV in the cover letter, which should expedite the job application process. E-mailed cover letters should have the same content as a printed cover letter, with the exception of the recipient's address. The phraseology should be consistent with a mailed letter. For example, the cover letter should start with 'Dear', not 'Hi', and include full contact details. As you will not know how compatible the recruiter's software and browser are with your own, here are some general e-mail cover letter guidelines which should be followed to minimize the effects of incompatible software.

Do not use:

☐ bullet points;
☐ underlining;
☐ bold or italic typeface;
☐ font colours;
☐ columns;
☐ heavy attachments of any other type than a Word document;
☐ attachments of PowerPoint, csv, txt, notepad, or any other file types that have to be zipped;
☐ graphics.

Do use:

☐ font size 10 or 12;
☐ Arial, Times Roman or Courier;
☐ non-zipped Word document attachments of maximum four pages in length;
☐ the vacancy reference number (if known) in the subject line of the e-mail, and the job title of the vacancy advertised, for example sales manager.

The box gives a sample e-mail cover letter.

E-mail cover letter example

Dear Sue,
I am writing in response to your advertisement for a direct sales teams manager as advertised on Workthing.com, reference: WT/1234.

You will see from my attached CV that I have more than two years' sales management experience in the accident and insurance sector. In particular I would like to draw your attention to my skills, knowledge and experience:

- [ ] Led a sales team of 10 to double turnover from £490,000 to £980,000 in one year.
- [ ] Coached two new recruits to team leader status in four months through agreed performance-based appraisals.
- [ ] Developed 'Close that deal' one-day seminar for all sales staff, and improved sales team performance by 10 per cent.

I would like to be given the opportunity to increase sales for your company, and nurture a formidable sales force to guarantee continuous business development.
 I may be contacted on:

E-mail: bob@hotmail.co.uk
Mobile: 07779 123 654

I look forward to hearing from you.
Regards,
Bob Jones.

21 Preston Road
Preston
Lancashire
LN2 4JY
01564 567890

UNDERSTAND THE COMPANY

Let us assume that you have already satisfied your work preferences as detailed in the job advertisement:

- [ ] work location: acceptable travel time to and from work;
- [ ] work type: office based, 9 to 5 or field work, irregular hours, shifts;
- [ ] employment type: permanent or contract, part time or full time, team work or individual work, job sharing, flexible hours.

Next you may want to consider how well you will fit the organizational culture. Most vacancy advertisements start with a description of the company. When you read the description you should consider your ideal working environment intermix (IWEI). An IWEI may consist of choices from the following:

- [ ] organization type: public or private sector, commercial or altruistic, large or small enterprise;
- [ ] organizational culture: bureaucratic or innovative;
- [ ] organizational structure: flat, with few department heads, or tall, with many department heads.

It is unlikely that you will be able to check the match with all your IWEI criteria just using the company description in the job advertisement. You may well need to research the company further. If the advertiser is using a recruitment consultancy to fill the position, the company name may not be shown. Usually the company is termed the 'client' in the text of the advertisement. If you cannot find out the company name, you may have to rely on the company description in the advertisement. There will be clues as to corporate culture in the advertisement regardless of whether or not the company is named.

If you do know the company or organization name, you should research the company by following the research tips covered in Chapter 3. If you do not know the name you could ask the recruitment consultant responsible – named as the contact in the advertisement – about the company. Ordinarily recruitment consultants will not name the company, but most will readily describe the company to you.

SPOKEN FIRST IMPRESSIONS

If you are in a situation where you are asked what you do, this could be a networking opportunity for you. It is advisable in such situations to have a 'story' to explain what you do in a jargon-free manner. A group of people who frequently have to explain complex facts and figures to non-practitioners is the staff of the National Audit Office. They have developed the 'dinner party' approach for just such occasions.

The dinner party approach

Dan Crabtree works for the National Audit Office (http://www.nao.gov.uk) as a Senior Auditor on the Public–Private Partnerships team. The National Audit Office (NAO) scrutinizes public spending on behalf of Parliament and is independent of government. The NAO audits the accounts of all government departments and agencies as well as a wide range of other public bodies, and reports to Parliament on the economy, efficiency and effectiveness with which government bodies have used public money.

The dinner party approach explained

Several years ago, the NAO developed what is known as the 'dinner party approach', which is designed to enable their work to be explained to a non-technical audience in a clear and punchy manner. The dinner party method can be used to explain a specific project you are working on, or it can also be used at a broader level to describe what you do, in a clear and concise fashion.

When is the dinner party approach used?

The dinner party takes place at the end of project fieldwork, as a forum for conversing with key players who were not involved in the detailed evidence gathering. It is very effective at cutting out waffle and irrational challenge, and allowing the report writers and client body to reach swift agreement on the structure of the final report. It may be that an individual or group has only a small involvement in one aspect of a large complex project, but the success of the project is dependent on everyone's 'buy in', no matter how small their involvement.

How is the dinner party approach applied?

Its output forms the basis of a written report, which is logical in structure. The logic that underpins the dinner party approach is SCQA: situation (the background to the issue), complication (what makes the subject interesting to look at), question (the obvious one that arises in the listener's or reader's mind) and answer (the solution to the problem).

So to put SCQA in the context of job hunting, the situation might be a business objective such as launching a new product. The complication might be that the company does not have anybody with the right skills set to launch the product. Talking to a potential recruit at a dinner party, the obvious question for the recruiter would be, 'Is this person the right candidate to take this product forward?' The answer would hopefully be yes – if the candidate knows about the recruiter's situation, complication and question.

Using the field social worker vacancy as an example, the dinner party approach might be applied like this:

- [ ] Situation: Company A needs to recruit a field social worker who has experience of working with young people and drug rehabilitation programmes in the public sector.
- [ ] Complication: Company A is a private sector company, which means that its mandate will be different from that of a public sector body.
- [ ] Question(s): Am I the right candidate for the job?
    - Do I understand Company A's mandate?
    - Do I know how performance is monitored?
    - Do I know what the local community's attitude towards illicit drugs is?
    - Do I know where the demand for Company A has come from?
    - Do I know how Company A is funded?
- [ ] Answer(s): The candidate is the right candidate because:
    - He/she has experience in achieving targets (performance monitoring).
    - The candidate has worked with local communities in the past to garner support.
    - The candidate is orientated towards the same goals as those of Company A, such as prevention and increased awareness of causes, through education.

How would this work as a conversation, as opposed to a response to an advertisement?

In response to the question 'What do you do?' the candidate might reply, 'I help communities cope with the effects of drug addiction through group and individual support. And I work with communities to prevent further addiction and rehabilitate addicts back to recovery.' This is very similar to a verbal profile statement: it has a clear focus on the benefit of what the individual does.

Where do the situation, complication, question and answer originate?

The SCQA structure stemmed from a desire to develop clear high-level conclusions from extensive evidence gathering. It complements a study design known as issue analysis, which is a rigorous structured approach for turning high-level questions, at project implementation stage, into specific audit tasks at the outset of a report.

What next for the dinner party approach?

The NAO is intending to produce a training film about the dinner party approach for the consumption of audit staff, who deal with complex projects on a day to day basis.

Now that you know how to talk and write about what you do, our attention shifts from the packaging to the contents. In the next chapter, different CV formats and types (online, printed, scanned and e-mailed) are explored, explained and exampled.

6 Write a winning CV

We can't all cry, 'Ding, dong, the CV's dead; ding, dong, the wicked CV's dead' just yet. For in the land beneath the rainbow the CV is still very much alive. This is because recruiters rely on CVs for screening purposes. If a CV gets screened in, the candidate is invited for an interview; if the CV gets screened out, it is filed.

So your ultimate goal must be to write a CV that will get you invited to interviews. Second to that, your penultimate aim should be to have your CV filed in the 'great candidate but not quite suitable for this job; keep for future vacancies' cabinet or database. Either way the content in your CV will determine the outcome. Assuming that you have done your homework to such an extent that you just know what a fantastic hire you would be, all that remains to be done is that you convey that in your CV. That means that your CV should demonstrate that you are Handy Andy, the fixer of all problems, the perfect person to run that employment market-stall.

RECRUITERS' CORNER

As there are so many dos associated with good CV writing it is simpler to start with the don'ts. So directly from recruiters' mouths, here are some major don'ts:

- ☐ Don't use niche jargon.
- ☐ Don't leave out your date of birth.
- ☐ Don't think that it's OK to send a 10-page CV because it's e-mailed.
- ☐ Don't detail anything that is irrelevant to the job.
- ☐ Don't attach a photograph.

☐ Don't use graphics, colours and features that cannot be scanned.
☐ Don't lie about experience, qualifications, skills (or previous convictions if asked).

Our career management pundits from Working Careers have assembled some top tips for effective CV writing. The key principles that should be applied to all CV composition are detailed in the box.

CV tips

Principal dos:

☐ Supply correct contact information.
☐ Pitch your CV at the target job or company.
☐ Keep it short and concise (maximum three pages).
☐ Put your name and preferred contact details (for example e-mail or mobile) at the top of every additional page (use full capitals).
☐ Stick to one of the three possible CV structures (chronological, combination or functional).
☐ Focus on results.
☐ Focus on achievements.
☐ Only include information that is relevant to the application.
☐ Spell and grammar check it.
☐ Include a full date-ordered career history (regardless of CV type).

And some more; a winning CV should include:

☐ A title first, which can be either your name or your generic job title (written in all uppercase).
☐ Personal details: first name, family name, address, correct contact details (day and evening phone numbers and an e-mail address).
☐ Personal profile: a short 'selling' statement about you (think market stall or Handy Andy).
☐ Employment: record employers' names, employment dates and job titles. (If you don't want your current employers to find out that you are job hunting, describe your current employer rather than naming it.)
☐ Achievements – should be results oriented.

- Responsibilities: focus on skills and strengths.
- Qualifications and skills, if relevant to the job and recent. Applicants aged over 25 may find that new skills are far more relevant to their job hunt. Skills, training or courses that have earned a certificate should definitely be detailed.
- Education: brief summary. If you are over 25 include only the highest qualification; if you are under 25 detail in full.
- Training: mention all training that is relevant to the job application, for example skills that have not earned a certificate.

And now for the don'ts:

- Don't entitle your CV 'curriculum vitae'.
- Don't leave gaps in chronology (regardless of CV type).
- Don't focus on responsibilities, without mentioning achievements.
- Don't describe your state of health. If your prospective employer health-screens, this can be done at a later stage.
- Don't specify your height and weight. If successful placement is dependent on height and weight ratios, the recruiter will assume you meet its requirements.
- Don't detail referees – contact details can be given later if requested.
- Don't mention family members' names or ages – this is irrelevant.
- Don't include marital status – it is irrelevant.
- Don't include salary requirements – this is better left until the job offer or interview stage.
- Don't give reasons for leaving your last or current job – this can be discussed at interview stage.

WRITING PROFILE STATEMENTS

As we indicated in the CV tips, a profile statement is the selling bit of your CV. It is the candidate's 'story' that Neil Lewis referred to in his interview about the hidden jobs market. Your profile statement should précis the benefit that you would bring to the organization. It is also predictably the bit of the CV on which candidates most often get stuck. This is exacerbated by its early position in the CV. If you are struggling to write your profile statement, start with the easy parts of your CV first: write down your work history, qualifications and contact details. Once you have written these down you should then be able to list your achievements (there were tips on how to do this in Chapter 1, and more tips follow below). Then you can approach your profile statement as if it was a summary of your CV. You should put the profile statement at the front of your CV beneath your contact details. See the box for suggested profile statements.

Sample profile statements

An experienced account administrator who works well under pressure to consistently meet strict deadlines. Enjoys working as part of a team or on own initiative using effective communication skills to achieve objectives.

A hardworking, reliable person with skills and experience in all aspects of customer service. Excellent attendance records and the ability to train inexperienced staff.

A professional and efficient secretary with several years' experience in operations and finance divisions. Excellent communication skills and attention to detail, also acknowledged for discretion, confidence and reliability.

A committed manager with proven people skills who is able to motivate staff to achieve high standards of customer service and sales performance.

A punctual and reliable long distance HGV driver, with over 10 years' long-haul experience and an exemplary safety record. (Examples provided courtesy of Working Careers)

To sum up, your profile statement should include common terminology such as a generic job title (like accounts administrator, HGV driver or secretary) and make reference to your area of expertise (customer service, finance division, sales performance). Your impetus for including a profile statement is to make the recruiter want to read the rest of your CV.

WRITING ACHIEVEMENTS

In defining your happy work realities you will already have explored your achievements, and understand what motivates you. The exercises in Chapter 1 should have helped you to realize what you are good at, what you enjoy doing and what your work preferences are. For a quick reminder of your work history and achievements you could refer to your career path drawing (see Chapter 2). If you do not have these exercises to refer to, then you should start by listing your work history by job titles, company name and to and from dates. For full-time permanent positions list up to three work histories. For interim, contract or part-time positions list up to 10 work histories, but try not to exceed a total CV length of three pages.

After listing your work histories take each job title in turn and categorize your responsibilities. Then for each of your responsibilities write down how you fulfilled them; this amounts to your achievements. Aim to use words that are results-focused. Typically the words used in a CV to describe achievements are action verbs. If you want your words to speak as loudly as your actions, you should use as many of these as possible. For a list of action verbs see Table 6.1.

Table 6.1   *Action words*

Arranged/planned	**Began/started**	**Changed/altered/ implemented**
Administered	Built	Combined
Arranged	Conceived	Conducted
Assembled	Constructed	Converted
Centralized	Created	Demonstrated
Decentralized	Devised	Developed
Complied	Established	Effected
Composed	Founded	Enacted
Coordinated	Generated	Executed
Designed	Initiated	Formulated
Developed	Installed	Modified

Table continued on next page

107

Organized
Planned
Prepared
Proposed
Scheduled

Instigated
Introduced
Launched
Originated
Piloted
Renewed
Set up

Negotiated
Processed
Produced
Redesigned
Redirected
Reengineered
Reorganized
Replaced
Restructured
Shaped
Transformed
Undertook
Utilized

Increased/made bigger
Accelerated
Broadened
Doubled
Enlarged
Exceeded
Expanded
Extended
Heightened
Strengthened
Surpassed
Tripled
Widened

Maintained
Conserved
Consolidated
Continued
Preserved
Supported
Sustained
Updated

Lessened/made smaller
Decreased
Halved
Lightened
Lowered
Minimized
Reduced
Shortened

Managed/controlled
Directed
Headed
Instructed
Led
Ordered
Piloted
Regulated
Steered
Supervised
Taught
Trained

Prevented/ended
Anticipated
Averted
Avoided
Completed
Diverted
Eliminated
Ended
Eradicated
Evaded
Finished
Forestalled
Halted
Liquidated
Prevented
Rejected
Stemmed
Stopped
Terminated

Researched/studied
Analysed
Appraised
Assessed
Audited
Calculated
Checked
Collated
Defined
Discovered
Estimated
Evaluated
Examined
Highlighted
Identified
Inspected
Investigated
Monitored
Probed
Projected
Proved
Surveyed
Tested
Uncovered
Verified

Suggested/advised
Approved
Counselled
Facilitated
Guided
Judged
Liaised
Prescribed
Prompted
Proposed
Recommended
Selected
Specified
Suggested

Urged
Encouraged
Inspired
Motivated
Spurred
Stimulated
Taught
Trained

Wrote
Documented
Drafted
Edited
Interpreted
Outlined
Publicized
Published
Revamped
Revised
Translated

(Source: courtesy of Working Careers)

When writing your achievements, focus on the benefit for your prospective employer. If you have enabled an organization to exceed its mandate, reduce costs, increase profit or productivity, then recruiters should want to speak to you, because you could increase the efficiency of their own organization.

How you present your CV to prospective employers is largely determined by the type of job seeker that you are. There are three types of CV: chronological (reversed), combination and functional (also known as skills based). The three different CV types draw attention to your career history and position it in relation to your next career move. They help you to anchor your career history within the context of your suitability to the position you are applying for. These CV formats are familiar to most recruiters, and they will recognize what you are saying about your skills and expertise by the way that you present them in your CV. For example the parent we used as an example in Chapter 2 should only detail her retail career history where it is relevant to teaching roles. A function or combination CV format would suit her particular career move better than a chronological CV format.

CV TYPES

Chronological CVs

This CV type is used by second jobbers or experienced hires, those who already have occupational experience relevant to the job they are applying for. The new job may represent a promotion or a specialist career move. The reverse chronology CV is not necessarily used for external applications only. For example some large organizations such as the Civil Service put out to tender new roles or projects, and first seek applications from within the organization. An existing employee could use a chronological CV to apply for such a position. Work history is provided in reverse order for a chronological CV, because the most recent role is considered the most relevant. For the layout of a chronological CV refer to the box.

Chronological CV layout

Personal details
Profile (optional)
Career/employment history (in reverse chronological order)
Achievements/responsibilities (highlight skills)
Qualifications/membership of professional bodies/focus groups
(where applicable)
Training
Education
Other relevant information (such as operational
experience/work experience/voluntary or charity work/rewards,
recommendations or commendations achieved/customer
testimonials/press cuttings).

(Example provided courtesy of Working Careers)

The next box shows how this layout can be applied to CV content.

Chronological CV with content

JO SMITH
59 Whiley Way
Hounslow
Middlesex
TW13 1XD
Tel: Day – 0207 123 4567 Evening – 0208 678 9012
Email: jo@aol.com

PROFILE
A well organized, reliable and commercially aware senior
manager with a wealth of experience in both large and small
companies. Enjoys pressure, accustomed to working to targets
and within given budgets. Strong ability to develop and
motivate others. Communicates comfortably and effectively at
all levels.

PROFILE SKILLS AND ACHIEVEMENTS
Managing Director, Facilities Maintenance Services Ltd,
1997–present

- ☐ Established Facilities Maintenance Services Ltd, building to six employees and a turnover of £520,000.
- ☐ Managed and controlled all staff recruitment and staff matters and ensured high levels of commitment and motivation.
- ☐ Planned and presented all financial accounts, accurately meeting tight deadlines including VAT and PAYE.
- ☐ Communicated with customers, ensuring exact requirements, maintaining high levels of customer service.
- ☐ Consistently achieved and maintained high standards supplying to food, beverages and telecommunications companies.

Sales Manager, Beta Bearings plc, 1993–1997

- ☐ Organized and managed sales for three branches within the London area.
- ☐ Developed and supervised a team of nine successful sales personnel.
- ☐ Actively involved in setting up new branches, including staff recruitment and training.

Senior Sales Engineer, CIG Bearing Co Ltd, 1987–1993

- ☐ Demonstrated excellent interpersonal skills when working with manufacturers, large end users and stockists.
- ☐ Built up sales base, met all sales targets and increased turnover.

Accounts Engineer, Cave Bros Co, 1983–1987

- ☐ Ensured all technical and commercial matters were met on home and export sales.
- ☐ Organized accounts for major motor manufacturers.
- ☐ Visited customers in UK and mainland Europe, building strong working relations.
- ☐ Represented companies at various trade shows.

Technical/Service Engineer, Dunestone, 1981–1983

☐ Completely resolved engineering production problems and tyre design modifications.
☐ Liaised with staff at all levels from operators to senior managers.

QUALIFICATIONS AND TRAINING

Product knowledge   HNC Mechanical Engineering
Sales techniques   City and Guilds Parts 1–3 Mechanical Engineering
Sales management   City and Guilds Mechanical Engineering
5 GCSEs

PERSONAL DETAILS

Date of birth 16/06/63

(Example provided courtesy of Working Careers)

Combination CVs

Combination CVs are so called because they combine work history or experience with skills. They are written in such a way as to highlight the applicant's occupational expertise. Combination CVs suit experienced hires, second jobbers, and in some cases career changers who want to make a lateral career move. This CV format enables a candidate to explain quickly why he or she would be capable of a role despite lacking time service experience in a precisely similar role. The combination CV therefore also lends itself to fast-track career moves.

If you have few years' experience but have amassed wide and varied expertise, then the combination CV may be for you. It can hold its own against chronological CVs that may demonstrate years of experience in a closely related role. As before, all highlighted skills and expertise should be relevant to the target job and company. See the boxes for a combination CV layout and an example of a combination CV.

Combination CV layout

Job title (generic)
Personal details
Objective (generic job title)
Summary (of work expertise history)
List five skills (evidence skills competence levels by detailing
results and achievements)
Experience (summarize work history and relate to skills
development as previously listed)
Education (summary)

Example of a combination CV with content

EMPLOYMENT SERVICES MANAGEMENT
Chris Smith
123 Anystreet
London NW1
0208 123 4444

OBJECTIVE:
Employment services management

SUMMARY: Ten years of increasing responsibilities in the
                employment services marketplace,
                concentrating in the high-technology markets.

SALES: Sold high-technology consulting services with
                consistently profitable margins throughout the
                United Kingdom. Grew sales from over
                £15 million to over £20 million per year.

PRODUCTION: Responsible for opening multiple offices and
                accountable for growth and profitability. One
                hundred per cent success and maintained

---

	30 per cent growth over a seven-year period in 10 offices.
MANAGEMENT:	Managed up to 40 people in sales, customer service, recruiting and administration. Turnover maintained below 14 per cent in a typically high turnover business. Hired branch managers, sales and recruiting staff throughout United Kingdom.
FINANCIAL:	Prepared quarterly and yearly forecasts. Presented, reviewed and defended these forecasts to the board of directors. Responsible for P & L of £20 million sales operation.
MARKETING:	Performed numerous market studies for multiple branch openings. Resolved feasibility of combining two sales offices. Study resulted in savings of over £5,000 per month in operating expenses.
EXPERIENCE:	Howard Systems International, Inc, 1997–Present Management consulting firm Personnel Manager Responsible for recruiting and managing consulting staff of five. Set up office and organized the recruitment, selection and hiring of consultants. Recruited all levels of MIS staff from financial to manufacturing markets. Additional responsibilities:

☐ Developed PR with industry periodicals – placement with over 20 magazines and newsletters.

☐ Developed effective referral programmes – referrals increased 320 per cent.

Technical Aid Corporation, 1989–1996
National consulting firm, Micro/Temps Division
Division Manager, 1995–1996
Area Manager, 1992–1995
Branch Manager,1989–1992

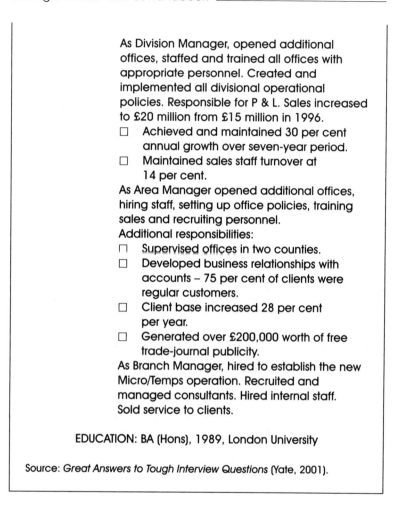

As Division Manager, opened additional offices, staffed and trained all offices with appropriate personnel. Created and implemented all divisional operational policies. Responsible for P & L. Sales increased to £20 million from £15 million in 1996.
- ☐ Achieved and maintained 30 per cent annual growth over seven-year period.
- ☐ Maintained sales staff turnover at 14 per cent.

As Area Manager opened additional offices, hiring staff, setting up office policies, training sales and recruiting personnel.
Additional responsibilities:
- ☐ Supervised offices in two counties.
- ☐ Developed business relationships with accounts – 75 per cent of clients were regular customers.
- ☐ Client base increased 28 per cent per year.
- ☐ Generated over £200,000 worth of free trade-journal publicity.

As Branch Manager, hired to establish the new Micro/Temps operation. Recruited and managed consultants. Hired internal staff. Sold service to clients.

EDUCATION: BA (Hons), 1989, London University

Source: *Great Answers to Tough Interview Questions* (Yate, 2001).

Functional or skills based CVs

The functional CV is best suited to first jobbers or complete career changers. This CV format showcases a candidate's transferable skills, and can be utilized where experience in a role is lacking. It is therefore important to demonstrate, when using a functional CV, that your willingness to learn has reduced costs, increased profits, helped an organization fulfil its mandate, and so on. Though it may be a safer choice for a recruiter to hire another candidate with specific work experience, that person is not guaranteed to do the job any better than you, so you must show that your attitude and approach to work produces results.

In addition, as organizations increasingly respond to changing markets, flexible staff play a key role in ensuring continuous business improvement. If you can establish that you have managed transition and quickly worked productively, then you will reduce the induction costs associated with new hires. As a candidate who can verify a positive response to change, you will increase your employability worth.

When using a functional CV, focus on substantiating how your attitude has proved successful in the past. You should also detail any work experience, voluntary work or professional body affiliations or memberships that could highlight your knowledge and expertise in a relevant discipline. For example, the parent used as an example in Chapter 2 could detail her involvement with her local parents' association. If you are a graduate, student or school leaver you could cite work experience, hobbies, interests, or voluntary work that you have undertaken, where skills have been honed. The boxed samples show a functional CV layout guide, an example of a functional CV, and an example of a graduate's functional CV expectant of graduation grade.

Functional CV layout

Personal details
Profile (optional)
Key skills/achievements (consider grouping)
Career/employment history (in outline)
Qualifications/memberships (if applicable)
Training
Education
Other information (such as voluntary work experience).

(Example provided courtesy of Working Careers)

Example of a functional CV with content

SHELLEY PRADA
12 Dane Street, Midwitch, Cheshire, S25 9EB
E-mail: shelley@hotmail.com Mobile: 08889 123456

Profile

An end-to-end supply chain management expert. Strengths lie in understanding and fulfilling the customers' needs. A resourceful and enthusiastic approach ensures increased productivity, increased profits, reduced costs and happy, motivated staff.

Key skills and achievements

Logistics
- Negotiated savings of £500k in 2002 from spend of £30 m (over and above value engineered design changes).
- Improved vendor base, eliminating exposure on critical items, and reduced material content of cost of sales from 55% to 47% in first year by total acquisition costing.
- Set up stock control activities to mobilize £800k of redundant stock (20% of total inherited stock was obsolete) and to ensure procedures were in place to prevent recurrence.

Materials
- Planned production of automated lines and organized the transfer of stocks and manufacturing activities to nominated sites.
- Implemented PC based line scheduling system to enable resource planning of materials, labour and decisions for subcontract/overtime to be taken in a planned manner.
- Introduced accountability for change with group companies by negotiating changeover dates and recharging write-off costs in addition to artwork origination charges.

Manufacturing services
- Implemented barcode tracking system of all operations with route cards to provide audit traceability to meet requirements.
- Developed and implemented electronic ordering system saving 6 weeks of a planner's time in manually performing MRP from up to 30 page parts lists.

☐ Created all procedures for manufacturing and materials to enable achievement of BS5750 accreditation.

Career summary

Galloway Ltd	**Logistics Manager**	1999–Present
Badar Production Ltd	**Materials Manager**	1996–1999
IB Ltd Manufacturing	**Services Manager**	1993–1996
FS Systems Ltd	**Materials Group Manager**	1992–1993
	Production Control Manager	1990–1992
The Greeting Foundation	**Production Control Manager**	1975–1990

Training and qualifications

Diploma Management Studies   HND Business Studies Distinction
Institute of Operations Management member
Health and Safety Risk Assessment

Systems experience

Computer Aided Design (CAD) Wireless Application Protocol (WAP)
Microsoft Excel (competent) Microsoft Office (proficient)
Lotus Notes 1, 2 & 3 (competent)

Personal details

Date of birth:	06/03/54
Interests:	Animal welfare, cooking and walking.

(Example provided courtesy of Working Careers)

Expectant of grade CVs enable graduates who have not yet qualified to apply for jobs, work experience and internships. If you are in your last year of university or college, you could utilize this CV format as a pre-qualified tool to counter seasonal employment competition (see the boxed example).

Graduate CV layout expectant of grade

Name
Address
Contact details: mobile and e-mail

Profile

Education

BA Marketing   Strathclyde University   2002–summer 2003
Expectant grade: 2:1 Hons

Areas of study

Dissertation
For example: Conducting an investigation into improving the competitiveness of Scottish companies in their domestic market. Due to contribute findings to a paper, which is being published by the *Journal of Strategic Marketing.*

Skills acquired
For example:
- ☐ Enhanced market research and analytical skills through interviewing marketing professionals of large blue chip companies about resolving their marketing issues.
- ☐ Improved communication skills. Assessed clients' needs and designed market research strategies. Analysed the collated data and wrote a marketing report for the company. The project group achieved second place out of ten short listed projects.

Key skills and achievements
Choosing up to five key skills and achievements, detail the following:
- ☐ What you did.
- ☐ How you did it.
- ☐ What skills you used.
- ☐ What you achieved.

Employment history
If applicable, list up to four work histories in the following way:
Job title   From – To   Company name

Training

IT expertise

Personal information

Date of birth:
Clean driving licence

Interests

Interests are important to a recruiter as they demonstrate your motivation, values and in some cases your intelligence. Remember that by writing too much it can send the signal that you have no time for work! An advisable amount of interests to list is three. Choose carefully as you may be asked about your interests at interview.

Self-employed CVs

If you are a freelancer, contractor, interim manager, or self-employed you might prefer to use a consultancy style CV format. This CV type can introduce your services to prospective clients without the need for a brochure or portfolio. If you are considering working for yourself, try experimenting with this CV format, as it will help you to formalize your business idea and the benefit that your services might bring to an organization. See the boxes for a consultancy CV layout guide and a consultancy CV with content example.

Self-employed CV layout

Personal details
Profile
Recent clients (if they cannot be named, describe them)
Key assignments undertaken
Qualifications
Memberships
Personal profile (background, business basis)

(Example provided courtesy of Working Careers)

Sample self-employed/consultancy CV with content

CLAIRE ANTHONY
19 Orchard Road, Romford, Essex, RM4 9SP
Tel: 01708 335708 E-mail: caconsultancy@compuserve.com

IT Project Manager with demonstrative success in systems analysis and design, business strategy development and operational planning in a variety of industries.

CLAIRE ANTHONY CONSULTANCY   1996–Present
Consultant to process reengineering companies – Various IT project management roles.
- ☐ Managed a small team of specialist project managers and engineers ensuring all major projects were delivered on time, within budget, to ISO9001 specifications.
- ☐ Introduced an operational planning and performance system which enabled consistency of delivery and resulted in £750k saving within 6 months.
- ☐ Gained competitive advantage by introducing benchmarking to all areas of the business having secured full board backing.
- ☐ Completed a wide range of projects in Eastern Europe and achieved Total Quality Management (TQM) award for management and achievement for a blue-chip organization.
- ☐ Designed and developed multimedia communication package to train new members of the project and reduce misunderstandings resulting from language difficulties.

BUSINESS CONSULTING LTD   1990–1996
Senior Consultant 1993–1996
- ☐ Managed a major project to design, develop and implement trading systems for a major investment bank. Following successful completion the system resulted in major savings in cost and transaction time.

Consultant 1990–1993
- ☐ Played a full role as a member of a team that carried out IT and process reengineering projects worldwide.

EDUCATION
Sussex University 1986–1990
BSc (Hons) Maths & Computer Science

TRAINING
Leadership in Action
Total Quality
    Management
Business Strategies

PERSONAL DETAILS
Date of Birth: 15.07.68
Interests and activities: Sports and reading

(Example provided courtesy of Working Careers)

ONLINE CVS

Online CVs are usually filled out in an application for a job via a job board, corporate site or recruitment consultancy site. Alternatively job seekers may complete online CVs and bank them in job board, corporate or recruitment consultancy CV databases. If you bank your CV into a job board CV database it will usually have a level of anonymity. This means that when recruiters search the CV database the contact details on the CV are ordinarily hidden from them. In the majority of cases contact with a candidate is made via proxy e-mail. The e-mail address of the candidate is hidden from the recruiter. That is why it is crucial that your e-mail address is correct on an online CV.

In addition, if you are currently employed in a permanent position, do not put the name of your current employer in the 'work history' part of your CV unless your current employer already knows that you are job hunting. If you do name your current employer in the work history section of your CV, there is a zillion to one chance that your boss might find your CV. You could ask your boss why he or she is searching for a replacement for you, but this is probably a conversation that you would rather not have. So unless you are comfortable with your job search being public, describe rather than name your current employer, for example as a large fashion retailer.

Some job boards allow candidates to choose zero anonymity, which means that candidate contact details are displayed in the recruiter's search results. A zero anonymity level suits graduates and school leavers, those who are unemployed and those whose job search is public. If you fall into any one of these groups you should name your last, or current, employer.

If you are job hunting, thinking of leaving, or would consider an appropriate job offer if it was presented to you, you should complete an online CV. Most online CVs take about half an hour to complete and there are several advantages to filling them out:

☐ Recruiters prefer online CVs because the format of applications is standardized, so your CV is more likely to be read.

☐ Recruiters can use CV search engines to match CVs to their requirements, so your CV is more likely to be found and read.

☐ Many fields are predefined, so completing the CV is relatively quick. Common categories include occupational group, industry sector, length of experience, job type (permanent/contract and so on) and qualification levels.

☐ The predefined fields should familiarize you with common job description terminology. This will help you when you write your CV.

☐ Usually the profile statement and skills can be cut and pasted into the CV.

☐ Once a CV is completed on a site it can be searched for by recruiters.

☐ Once a CV is completed on a site it can be used to apply for more than one job on the same site.

☐ Some job boards (http://peoplebank.com) produce print copies of online CVs.

A slight disadvantage of online CVs is inconsistency. Online CVs are a relatively new phenomenon: some of the first online CV databases were created in the mid-1990s in America and Australia. As CV database technology evolved, so too has the format of the online CV. Unfortunately this means that you are likely to have to fill out several different types of online CV. In addition, most online CVs are a mixture of free text and predefined data fields. The fields are constructed in such a way as to retrieve the most accurate search results for the recruiter.

When completing your CV, you need to ensure that it will be found by the recruiter's CV search engine. The types of fields that exist in an online CV determine the way the search engine works. If when filling out your CV you notice that the fields are predominantly predefined, it means that the search is narrow and will only find 'exact' predefined matches.

When choosing a predefined category (such as occupational grouping) choose a broad description such as a generic job title. If you are able to multiple select (pick more than one definition) then you should do so. So your job title might read: sales manager, account handler, sales executive, senior sales, client relationship manager. By making a wider selection you will increase the probability that your CV will be found by a prospective employer.

Free text fields match on similar words or combinations of words. The search functionality is similar to that of keyword searching. The most common free text fields in online CVs are the profile statement, interests and skills fields. As the search matches to the word typed in by the recruiter, your aim should be to use similar words to those used by recruiters, so that your CV is found. This also means that if you make a typing error when inputting words into a free text field, your CV may not be keyword matched. Most online CVs do not have an automated spell or grammar check, so you should check for errors before submitting your CV.

In order to get the greatest benefit out of your online CV, you should use broad predefined categories, and describe skills and achievements using as many similar meaning words as possible. See the box for tips on writing online CV content.

Tips for writing online CVs

Job title	Sales Manager	(predefined)
Industry	Media	(predefined)
Experience	3 years	(predefined)
Achievements		(free text)

Managed a large sales team of 17 advertising executives. Responsible for launch of two new publications. Liaised with

---

editorial and creative teams to ensure dynamic content. Devolved management style to account handlers so that client spend was doubled. Clients included media companies such as Saatchi and Saatchi, Claritas EU and Ogilvy Interactive, and corporates such as IBM, British Airways (BA), British Broadcasting Company (BBC) and American Express.

In the example the word 'manage' has been expanded and used as manager, managed and management. The candidate has used the words advertising, media, creative, editorial, and several media company brand names in his achievements description. He has written in full company names and used the correct abbreviations. In this way a keyword search on 'manage' or 'media' should retrieve this CV, as would a keyword search on 'BA' or 'British Airways'.

If you are detailing IT skills you should write the name of the program or software in full, and also use the recognized abbreviation. For example write: 'Microsoft Certified Systems Engineer' and 'MCSE'. In this example a search on either MCSE or Microsoft Certified should find this CV. Use the correct spelling: for example 'Microsoft PowerPoint' is spelt correctly but 'PowerPoints' is misspelt.

SCANNABLE CVS

The CVs featured in most of the examples in this chapter would be suitable as printed CVs. If the CVs were to be scanned once received, they might not function as well. Recruiters and hiring managers tend to be constrained by the human resource management (HRM) system they have. Some HRM systems rely on scannable CVs. It is only once a CV has been scanned into the recruiter's database that the CV can be read by the HRM system. Scanned CVs are read by keyword matching software, so the principles that increase the likelihood of free text fields in online CVs being found are equally applicable for scanned CVs.

As a scanned CV is *all* free text, you should endeavour to use similar generic job titles to those used in your profile statement and work history. If you are mailing a CV to a prospective employer there are a few simple rules that you should follow to make sure that your CV is scannable. Stick to:

- [ ] plain and common type fonts such as Arial, Times, Courier, Optima and Palatino;
- [ ] font sizes between 10 and 14;
- [ ] asterisks, minus, less than, plus signs or approximates to be used as bullet points. The symbols for the words above look like this: * – < + (shown in the same order as listed).
- [ ] white or beige A4 paper;
- [ ] original copies;
- [ ] a laser jet printer.

Avoid:

- [ ] folding or stapling your CV;
- [ ] heavily stylized designs;
- [ ] odd font sizes (such as 11 and 13);
- [ ] Tahoma, Batang, Verdana or Gothic font types;
- [ ] automated bullet points;
- [ ] columns and vertical lines;
- [ ] italic typeface;
- [ ] automated headers or footers;
- [ ] too much use of bold type.

Good CV practices still apply. Ideally your CV should be no more than two pages long, and your name should appear first on every consecutive page. Follow the ideal CV format, combination, chronological or functional, for the type of career move that you are making.

CVS AS ATTACHMENTS

If you are asked to e-mail your CV to a recruiter, then invariably the recruiter will use a keyword search to find suitable CVs. This again relies on the recruiter's HRM system being able to read your CV. As with scanned CVs, if your CV attachment is heavily stylized a computer may not be able to read it. In addition if you have written your CV in the latest Office software it may contain new features that are incompatible with the recruiter's Office software. Another factor in the readability of emailed CVs is browser compatibility. Examples of common browsers include Outlook, Netscape and Internet Explorer. Incompatible browsers can reformat e-mails and hide or alter text. So when you write your CV, try to adhere to the scannable CV rules, which should negate the effects of incompatible browsers.

It may be that there is more than one role that could provide your next career move. If this is the case you may need to write more than one CV, having one for each possible role. Alternatively you could use a targeted cover letter to verify and highlight the matches in your CV to the employer's requirements. If you choose this approach you should need one generic CV only. You can find more CV inspiration, tips and ideas online and in books. For a guide to online CV tips and examples, and a list of CV books with synopses, see Appendix 1.

When talking CVs, just like ruby slippers, one size does not fit all. If your CV is targeted, it is more likely to facilitate the recruiter's decision to screen it in. Though it is time consuming to write your first CV, once completed it can be updated quickly. It is good practice to revisit your CV whenever you achieve something new or commendable at work, and during appraisal times. Keeping your CV accurate will help you to remain focused on making the right career moves. By writing a short and concise CV that is two to three pages in length, you should have plenty to talk about at the interview stage.

7 Know what recruiters are looking for

Knowing what recruiters are looking for need not be like going on a treasure hunt where Einstein has set the clues. Probably the best way to understand their requirements is to ask them what differentiates those candidates who get shortlisted and selected from those who do not. In this chapter we feature interviews with some of the UK's big volume recruiters. To help you to also look the part we will be passing on style tips in our interview with fashion guru Paul Thomas, from one of the Arcadia Group's flagship Topman stores.

RECRUITERS' CORNER

In vogue

Jane Norman is the Training Programmes Manager of the Arcadia Group's management trainee programmes. The Arcadia Group (http://www.arcadiagroup.co.uk) is the UK's second largest fashion retailer, employing over 24,000 people and operating in 2,000 stores nationwide. The group is the name behind the leading high street brands Burton, Dorothy Perkins, Miss Selfridge, Evans Outfit, Topshop, Topman and Wallis. In the interview below Jane spotlights what is in vogue for fashion retail recruiters.

What are the entry-level qualifications for the fashion retail sector?

Fashion retail is one of the fastest growing industries in the world today, providing its employees with a huge variety of challenges, successes and new responsibilities. Opportunities start at 16, with the option of

becoming a sales adviser in a store after completing GCSEs. If candidates are looking for fast-track development opportunities they will generally need A levels or equivalent qualifications at 18 plus, and a degree at graduate entry level. Candidates who want to enter a specific function within fashion retail such as finance or buying may find that companies request a finance or fashion-related degree. Candidates should look out for this when making decisions on which company to apply for a position with.

Qualifications are highly valued and sought after in fashion retail, as is experience. At the Arcadia Group we value talented individuals who have a real passion to work in the industry.

What training and development would a candidate receive in your sector?

Training and development can include anything from straightforward day to day, on the job training to structured development programmes and support for professional qualifications. Every company is different, although generally development will be based around a set of competencies that are specific to industry needs. Examples include customer focus, commercial awareness, communication, and product or brand knowledge.

Research conducted on graduates and school leavers such as the UK Graduates' Careers Survey 2002 (14,000 graduates were surveyed) supports the belief that candidates value structured training and development with real responsibilities. The Arcadia Group's Retail Management Trainee Programmes offer a range of on and off job development activities that support the individual in achieving transferable skills. These include team leadership and management workshops, business projects and assignments, which are all supported by continuous reviews on progress.

We have also developed an exclusive Management Trainee Programme (MTP) for school leavers with two A levels (or their equivalent) and five or more GCSEs. The MTP is a 12-month store-based development programme where trainees gain 'hands on' experience and learn how to manage a store and its team. On successful completion of the programme, a trainee is promoted to store manager. The opportunity to further develop the skills and attributes required for successful business management continues: we have promoted MTP employees to senior management positions within three to five years.

The Arcadia Group also offers a graduate three-year Retail Management Development Programme, which is tailored for HND/degree students. Arcadia receives over 6,000 enquiries a year

from students who aspire to manage their own store. The ultimate aim of the Graduate Programme is for us to find high calibre graduates who will be our area managers of the future.

Though it would depend on the size of the company, candidates may find that opportunities are not restricted to the shop floor alone. We also recruit graduates into head office positions. Examples of head office careers include distribution, merchandising and positions in finance.

Where can candidates find fashion retail sector jobs?

Candidates should watch out for in-store advertising for local opportunities, and also major nationwide campaigns. Some companies may have in-house recruitment teams, and also use Internet advertising or agencies as a source to attract candidates.

At the Arcadia Group we operate promotional campaigns for each of our recruitment programmes. We highlight the career opportunities that are available to students. Our Internet site is a popular job source for candidates {see http://www.arcadiagroup.co.uk/promostores/arcadia/gr/}. In addition candidates should check key student publications for job opportunities.

However, we believe that you cannot beat face to face meetings, so we are always out and about discussing career opportunities with candidates at colleges and universities. We also invite trainees and graduates from previous years to share their success stories at the events that we attend.

Most companies benchmark their salaries alongside other retailers in the sector, so candidates should also consider additional benefits such as career development opportunities. We strive to provide fantastic fashion retail career paths at Arcadia, and were recently voted Employer of Choice for Graduates seeking a career in Retail (UK Graduates' Career Survey 2002).

What do you look for when recruiting/interviewing a prospective candidate?

Above all it is about having the ability to demonstrate a passion for the customer and the industry. 'The customer is King' may be a cliché – but without them we wouldn't have a business. An interview is the foundation stone for whatever job level a candidate is applying for. A company may expect its potential employee to demonstrate any of the following skills and attributes (and maybe more!):

- ☐ an element of business acumen;
- ☐ good communication skills;
- ☐ examples of working with and supporting others;
- ☐ analytical or problem solving skills;
- ☐ an eye for detail or creativity;
- ☐ a focus on achieving or getting a good result;
- ☐ determination, use of initiative and enthusiasm.

As with any company, at Arcadia we shape the interview to reflect the technical and personal skills we require for the candidate to be successful in the role. However, the most impressive candidates are the ones who can show their eagerness to work for our business. They do this by researching the role they are applying for, so that they really understand what it means. For example, being a distributor for Topshop is not about driving a lorry! It involves planning and allocating hundreds of thousands of pounds of stock, and ensuring the stores receive it on time and within budget.

On a personal note, I have had an amazing career in this industry. It has offered me, and continues to offer me, opportunities that I never even imagined. At a time when some employment markets have experienced great unrest, mine is an industry with credibility, longevity and healthy future expansion prospects.

Singing for supper

Mike Stapleton, UK Corporate Affairs Manager, details how candidates can enter the contract food service sector, and the interview/audition process at Compass Group (http://www.compass-group.com).

What are the expected entry-level qualifications for the contract food service market?

Expected entry-level qualifications vary depending on the programme applied for. For our chef's development programme the entry-level qualifications are an NVQ level 2 or 3 in professional cookery. We also actively recruit school leavers and train them to NVQ level 2 or 3 standards in a range of topics. The training is conducted either via our Modern Apprenticeship schemes or in-house programmes. From there candidates can choose whether or not they would like to enter the chef's development programme.

At Compass Group recruits start at a level that befits their qualifications; we do not see any benefit in making graduates or executives reinvent the wheel. We employ them for their skills and potential, and from day one we look to move them forward through mentorship, coaching, training and development. Retention and development of great people is key to our agenda.

What is the 'audition' process at Compass Group?

We prefer to audition rather than interview candidates because factors such as social skills, personality, presentation and attitude are key to the supply of our services to clients. These factors very much affect clients' satisfaction levels and set the standard for high quality customer care. We have good training and development programmes for these areas, but their success is very dependent on candidates' willingness and ability to participate. Therefore we look at the 'whole person' not just from the point of view of the job that they are applying for today, but also the promoted role that they may aspire to. Taking a longer term, succession planning view is extremely important to us.

It is also commonly known that the majority of people do not perform to their best ability during formal interviews. We have created a more relaxed interview environment, which facilitates an exploratory approach. This has enabled us to evaluate a range of candidate abilities and uncover a candidate's natural strengths and weaknesses. This assists us in defining a development programme for candidates, which commences on the candidate's placement with us.

Formal qualifications do not necessarily determine good performance. Experience and attitude may contribute more towards better performance, and hence we welcome applications from both background types. A mixture of these two background types is usually the elixir of good and consistent performance. But when we recognize potential we are very happy to invest in it, and enjoy the results of recruiting such a candidate.

How does a candidate 'get the part' with Compass Group?

Our industry is exciting, vibrant and varied, yet clients often have quite conservative demands from the people that provide services to them. Furthermore our clients' perceptions of the services that we provide are mainly formed by the people that they interface with. This is similar to the relationship that a hotel client has when speaking to the reservationist on the telephone or the doorperson on arrival. How people appear, present themselves, act and interact often predetermines client satisfaction levels.

Therefore using practical and verbal exercises at the interview helps to highlight these candidate facets. It also assists us in identifying the 'real person', and usually facilitates candidates demonstrating and giving their best.

What would impress you about a candidate?

An aura of enthusiasm along with an upbeat personality and logical thought processes are usually extremely impressive. We also look out for signs of a committed attitude. This is usually detected through candidates presenting themselves neatly and tidily for interview. We feel that this demonstrates effort, respect and a good level of self-esteem.

When candidates are confident and considered in their response to questions, and interact with their interviewers and fellow applicants in the same way, we are generally impressed. Similarly, the fact that a candidate has done some research about who the company is and what they do and how he or she would fit in, both now and in the future, are impressive attributes. Above all honesty and sincerity are irresistible!

Constructive advice

Tony Welch, HR Director from Galliford Try plc (http://www.gallifordtry. plc.uk), unfolds career paths within the contract construction sector, and details what candidate attributes impress him.

What are the entry-level qualifications for the contract construction sector?

For construction operatives there is no minimum entry level. We train these recruits to NVQ levels 1 and 2, which takes two years. Craftspeople such as carpenters receive three years' training to achieve an NVQ level 3. The entry level for site managers is four GCSEs, grade Cs or above; recruits receive three years' training up to NVQ level 3 and 4. Graduates would enter the industry and be examined in one of three disciplines: civil engineering, quantity surveying or Chartered Institute of Building. Galliford Try also employs people in traditional roles such as purchasing, marketing, IT, administration, finance and accounts, customer care and communications.

What would impress you about a candidate's application?

We look out for individual letters of application, which are targeted at the company and position or role that is being applied for. We would expect a high standard of CV that followed a familiar format. A high standard of CV is one that is free from spelling mistakes and grammatical errors and has a logical structure. It should be relevant to the position that is being applied for and not exceed three pages in length. We would want to see achievements highlighted in the CV: this tells us more about a candidate's ability to do the job than a list of work histories and responsibilities.

What differentiates candidates at the interview stage?

Regardless of the level of the vacancy, whether for a qualified or senior position, or unqualified or junior position, candidates should endeavour to be presentable. Obviously not everybody can afford a suit, but we like to see our interviewees smartly dressed. If the interview is for a more senior position, we would expect the candidate to dress according to the role that he or she hopes to fulfil.

As the interview stage is ordinarily the first time we meet a candidate, we appreciate punctuality. Construction is very timely work, so punctuality is important.

During the interview, candidates would earn brownie points for having researched our company site and for having an awareness of our business. As we have a clear focus on knowledge sharing we like to recruit candidates who are interested in lifelong learning. If a candidate is able to discuss the training that we offer, we would take that as an indication that the candidate would be suited to a learning culture such as ours. When candidates bring a list of questions to the interview this is also impressive; it shows that they have thought beyond the application stage on to how they would do the job.

Obviously if candidates are pleasant and smile this makes the whole process a lot more enjoyable.

Commodity careers

Mary Whitaker, HR expert from UBS Warburg (www.ubswarburg.com), describes investment banking careers from start to finish.

What are the entry-level qualifications for investment bankers and other roles at UBS Warburg?

For experienced hires, requirements differ dependent on the role. The Investment Banking Department looks for impeccable academic credentials but also beyond educational qualifications alone. Candidates must have a proven track record of achievement in their previous work experience, whether within investment banking, other professions such as law, accountancy, or any other relevant industry.

In other business areas, requirements may include a specific skill set – being a graduate isn't always a necessary prerequisite. For each role that we have, we clearly highlight the minimum requirements such as 'qualified chartered accountant' or 'must have HR administration experience within a blue chip/corporate environment' – it all depends on the role.

What differentiates candidates for UBS Warburg?

We encourage our people to contribute to an organization that is well known for its flat reporting structure and global lines of communication. A career at UBS Warburg is all about individuality and choice. We seek out people who are persistent, creative and possess a strong work ethic; individuals who understand the power of teamwork and who constantly challenge accepted wisdom; those who are looking for more than just a job. In return the opportunities for lateral and promotional career development at UBS Warburg are limited by the candidate's aspirations and determination only.

We expect candidates to know as much as possible about UBS and the industry, much of which can be gained from our Web site and other sources.

How do you assess candidates' suitability?

Each recruitment process starts with the definition of the open position and a role profile. At UBS Warburg we structure the interview around the bank's competency model. Competency based interviews ensure that candidates are assessed against relevant performance criteria, and hence enable greater objectivity in the interviewing process. Candidates will have at least two line manager interviews and an HR interview. In some areas the recruitment process also includes testing, whether technical or psychometric. Assessment centres are also used, although predominately this is for graduate recruitment.

Food for thought

Barbara Firth, Nestlé UK (http://www.nestle.co.uk) York site Recruitment Manager, outlines how Nestlé people build business.

What typifies Nestlé employees?

We believe in people rather than systems: great businesses are built by great people. We uphold continuous improvement (CI), which is a philosophy that works on the principle of 'what we do well today, we can do better tomorrow'. All of our employees, whatever their role, are encouraged to question how they do things with a view to improving processes and creativity. They are assisted with taking calculated risks and learning from their experiences. We champion lifelong learning and have an extensive Learning and Development portfolio that supports individuals in making the most of their potential.

Playing soft-ball

Janet McGlaughlin is the Operations Director of Pertemps Recruitment Partnership (http://www.pertemps.co.uk). She shares her experienced views on what recruiters want with us.

What do your clients say they want from candidates?

We work with clients towards developing processes that ensure that the decision to employ someone is based on objectivity and fairness. We employ a number of recruitment tools including psychometric evaluation, competency and biographical interview, and an assessment of hard skills such as IT literacy levels. This is partly done so that we satisfy our client's remit. In addition at Pertemps we interview and screen all of our candidates, so that we can investigate career options with them and highlight their transferable skills and work preferences so that we match the right candidates to the right jobs.

What soft skills are in demand?

We are finding that employers want candidates who are willing to learn. This is largely because roles can evolve very rapidly, and companies and organizations need employees who can learn quickly, manage change and multitask. In addition, as there is now so much readily available information, good judgement and initiative are important personality traits for candidates whose roles involve research, analysis or learning. The usual soft skills of negotiation, influencing and communication are still in great demand.

What the doctor ordered

GlaxoSmithKline (www.gsk.com), the international pharmaceutical and consumer healthcare company, recently developed a careers area for its site. We asked how this had affected the hiring practice.

How has the careers area of your site affected the way that you recruit?

It's faster, and candidates can visit the site, see what vacancies we have, and what sorts of people we employ. It has meant that we are receiving applications for many different roles within GSK from candidates at all stages of their career development. This has been a positive result for us, as we wanted candidates to become aware of the different career opportunities within GSK and preferably apply for them via our site.

When we did our last round of graduate internships we based a short screening questionnaire on information that could be found on the site. The graduates who performed really well had researched the site carefully. This sort of self-selection helps both candidates and recruiters, because the more candidates know about an organization, the more they understand what the job would be like. From a recruiter's perspective it shows enthusiasm, interest and that the candidate spent time applying for the job. These are all attributes that recruiters should recognize and value; we certainly do at GSK.

We are now operating an online recruitment process. If employees want to make lateral, internal career moves, we can match them to new jobs more easily. Candidates should spend just as much time on preparing an online CV as they would a printed CV. There needs to be enough relevant information in a CV for a recruiter to be able to decide whether to invite the candidate for an interview or not. Also it may be that the applicant does not quite have the rights skills or knowledge for the advertised job, but we would always look at a good CV and consider whether the applicant was suitable for another position.

Would you expect candidates to send an online cover letter with their online CV?

No, a cover letter is not always necessary if it duplicates what is in the CV. If a recruiter has actually stipulated that he or she wants a cover letter then the applicant should send one, but otherwise it shouldn't count against the candidate.

You mentioned graduate internships earlier on. What sort of internships do you offer?

In the UK we have a wide range of industrial placement and graduate programme opportunities for graduates and postgraduates in research and development, global manufacturing and supply, general management MBAs, IT, finance, procurement and sales and marketing.

The placement opportunities run throughout the year and can be applied for via the GSK site (http://www.gsk.com). We advertise all our current vacancies on our site so that candidates may apply for suitable positions.

Where can graduates find out about internships or work placements?

They can find out about them at graduate recruitment fairs or corporate sites. Again we would recommend that graduates visit corporate sites to research their target companies and placement opportunities first, before they apply for jobs or placements.

What are your predictions for e-recruitment?

Web sites are a growing medium, and more and more companies are developing the careers areas of their Web sites. We would recommend that candidates develop a good electronic CV, as increasingly companies are recruiting online.

LOOK THE PART

Advice from a trend advisor

Paul Thomas is a Trend Advisor at the Oxford Circus Topman store (http://www.Topman.co.uk). Trend advisors were first introduced in eight city-located Topman stores in the autumn of 2002. Topshop (http://www.Topshop.co.uk), a Topman sister company, has employed style advisors in city-based stores since autumn 2001. Trend and style advisors provide free personal dressing advice to shoppers.

Who uses trend advisors?

Men mainly, because we're a male fashion shop. Although Debenhams have personal shoppers in their suiting department, I am not aware of any other high street retail chain that provides personal dressing advice to men. We have individual customers who want a whole new wardrobe, and we have customers that want one outfit or one item: they might be going to a party, on a date or to an interview. We also have customers who have received a gift and don't know what to wear with it:

their girlfriend might have bought them some combats and they don't know what style of shoes to wear with them.

We advise partially sighted individuals and also those that are colour-blind if they need our help with matching colours and clothing. We also work closely with celebrities' stylists. Some celebrities like to shop here themselves. We work with stylists from *Pop Idol*, *Blind Date*, children's television shows, *Family Affairs*, *EastEnders*, comedy shows, and with music stylists for bands like So Solid Crew. We don't have typical trend advisor customers; all sorts of people like advice on their appearance.

What general dressing tips would you give to people?

It is much easier if you see the person and get to work with him and try things on, but in general our advice would be this. If you are short:

- [ ] wear fitted, tailored clothing;
- [ ] avoid horizontal stripes or bold patterns – they will make you look wider or squatter;
- [ ] wear bootleg cut trousers – they will make your legs look longer.

If you are tall:

- [ ] avoid vertical stripes – they will elongate your shape.

If you have wide hips:

- [ ] (women) wear bootleg cut, hipster trousers – the bootleg cut balances out the width of the hips, and the lower waist serves to lengthen the waistline, so that hips appear smaller;
- [ ] (men) avoid trousers with a high or gathered waist line.

Both men and women should:

- [ ] experiment with colours – it is usually the shade of the colour that determines whether or not it suits someone;
- [ ] wear jackets that finish at a third thigh length – they tend to be more flattering.

How would you advise candidates to dress for interview?

It does depend a little on what type of a job they are applying for. If the job is in fashion retail or media entertainment they probably don't need to wear a formal suit. For these types of interviews male candidates could still look presentable in a jacket and jeans with shoes. We would recommend that candidates avoid normal trainers. If a candidate were to go for an interview to work in a bank, we would advise him to wear a suit. Fashionable suits always look good, and it shows the interviewer that the candidate has taken care of his appearance.

In general candidates should demonstrate that they have taken care over their appearance, and reflect the culture of the organization in how they present themselves. If a candidate cannot afford a suit, coordinated separates (jackets and skirts or trousers) can look as smart as a suit and are usually less expensive. If candidates do wear jewellery that's part of them, and we would recommend that they wear it to interview. If they are working in a sports and leisure or catering environment, they will know that they need to remove or cover jewellery up.

What did you wear to your interview for the trend advisor position?

I wore a black and white pinstriped mod suit, with a lemon yellow shirt, shoes and a black tie that I'd made myself. I like suits and as the recruiters were spending time interviewing me, I thought that it was important to show my appreciation and respect of that in the way that I dressed.

Are Topman and Topshop fashions too young for some?

We have several concessions within Topman. Our Vintage range is aimed at 30s plus and features classics, and we have our funky ranges like Void for example. The emphasis at Topman and Topshop is on stylish, fashionable, affordable clothing. If a person were to go for an interview we would recommend that he or she should aim to look with it and up to date. The advice that we give to customers about what suits them best is service based; they can use the advice that we give them to buy clothes from any retailer.

SUMMARY

There were two resounding themes throughout 'Recruiters' corner'. The first attitudinal theme is enthusiasm. It would seem that this attribute above any other is what convinces recruiters that candidates can and will do the job. Although entry-level qualifications were discussed, lack of experience, it would appear, can be countered by a willingness to learn.

The second theme was research. Candidates who researched companies appeared to be more interested in the job than those who did not. So if you want to wow recruiters it is advisable to research your company, demonstrate a learning and enthusiastic attitude, which enables you to stay abreast of changes and contribute significantly to the organization from day one.

8 Make the grade

Entrance level tests have long been associated with recruitment and selection for senior positions, highly specialized roles, and the emergency services and armed forces. Additionally, the recent downsizing of IT departments in response to dot.com busts and declining technology markets has led many hiring managers to test the IT skills of applicants. Attainment levels are tested to ensure that recruits have the IT skills sets they claim to have.

It is not just for these sectors and roles, however, that selection tests or questionnaires are set. Increasingly companies are using selection tests to improve the probability of hiring people who can and will do the job. Selection tests are now commonplace in the recruitment process. Indeed there is a growing tendency to ask candidates to complete competency, personality or psychometric tests among search and selection consultancies.

We were introduced to popular selection tests in Chapter 1, where it was suggested that job seekers familiarize themselves with these tests. This is because it is very likely that you will be asked to complete a test during the course of job seeking. To prepare you for this and help reduce nerve twinges, panic attacks or tidal waves of overwhelming terror, we have asked David Millner, a professional test author, for his thoughts on the subject.

Ask an expert

We first met David in Chapter 1, where he shared his personality questionnaire expertise with us. To briefly reintroduce him, David Millner is the Consultancy Services Director of Psychometric Services Ltd (PSL). As such he assists HR experts and line managers with job analysis, the development of competency profiles, the creation of assessment methodologies and the design of assessment centres.

What sorts of companies use competency questionnaires or ability tests?

Most large corporates and mid-sized businesses use competency questionnaires or ability tests. They use tests because effective screening reduces staff churn (staff leaving) and the cost to hire. Organizations and companies invest time and money in hiring, such as the cost of advertising, and the time involved in managing responses and interviewing. Then when a candidate is recruited he or she typically undergoes an induction or training stage. This can take anything from one day to several months. While a new recruit is learning the trade he or she is not as productive as a fully trained coworker. If a recruit leaves during, or shortly after, the probationary period, the employer has made a substantial financial investment for little return. That's why increasingly companies are using more scientific selection methods. Competency questionnaires and ability tests can reduce churn, because candidates are assessed in terms of their match to the job, so ideally if a test is used the candidates who match the role demand should be better at doing the job than those who don't.

If a company uses tests as part of a selection process, it first has to decide who its ideal recruit would be. The test is designed and written to meet the recruitment requirements. It is validated to ensure that it measures what the organization is looking for in candidates, then company employees are trained on how to administer the tests and assess test results. This is quite a lengthy and relatively expensive process.

For small companies the cost of training test administrators often precludes the use of tests. There may also be a perception in small enterprises that selection tests are not needed, that employers know who their ideal recruits would be without the need of tests. In general in small organizations that typically do not have HR or personnel departments, there is a lack of understanding of their usage.

What do companies use the tests for?

The primary use for the tests is to provide an indication of an individual's ability to the recruiter. Competency and ability tests can be used to recruit according to an organization's key performance indicators (KPIs). For example a sales operation may have a KPI that states that sales people should be undeterred by rejection, so that if a prospective customer says 'No' to them, they move on to another prospect. There are competency and psychometric questions that indicate an individual's propensity to fulfil this KPI.

Also, even though most organizations pay market rate wages for their staff they want value for money, so they want to recruit better candidates than their competitors. An individual who is well suited to the job is likely to be more productive than another less well suited individual, so it makes commercial sense for organizations to use selection tests. These tests can reduce churn and increase companies' return on investment in human capital (employees).

At what stage are the tests used?

Mainly at the recruitment or internal selection stage, but occasionally tests are used for succession planning and developmental purposes. Some organizations use selection tests throughout an employee's career within the organization. In such organizations, if an employee were to apply for a promotion or specialist role, he or she could be assessed for his or her suitability for the role. These organizations tend to use predefined competencies to appraise their employees also. The purpose of these tests is to monitor and assist an employee's personal development through a competency-based human resources management model.

When should a candidate expect to take a test like this?

To start with there are, broadly speaking, three types of tests that a candidate might be asked to take. There are killer or screening questions such as 'Do you have a clean driving licence?' and 'Are you permitted to work in the UK?' These sorts of question usually have yes/no answers. In general if candidates do not give the right answers they are screened out and not shortlisted or invited for interview. Killer questions are most often put to candidates online, or sometimes over the phone. Killer questions are asked either when the candidate applies for a job, particularly if the job is advertised online, or shortly after the recruiter receives the candidate's application. In terms of screening tests, psychometrics, which measure mental capacity or intelligence, are most commonly used. They are largely used for sifting purposes, and can replace the first interview. Although there are few screening tests on the market, their usage is mainly as an online sifting tool.

The second type of tests are ability tests. These establish a candidate's level of attainment in a given discipline: Java development, numeric ability, verbal reasoning and so on. In most cases ability tests are set at the interview stage or as part of a selection day or weekend. Some organizations ask candidates to take ability tests a couple of days before their interview; this is so that the results can be discussed during the interview. A candidate could be asked to take a short online test at the time of applying for a job, or called and asked some questions over the phone.

The third test type is the competency questionnaire. Once again, although these can be delivered online or over the phone, they are most commonly delivered at the interview stage or as part of a selection day or weekend. Occasionally candidates are asked to complete competency tests a few days before the interview so that the results can be explored as part of the interview. (See the boxed example on page 149 for interview guidelines based on the results of a competency questionnaire.)

We would recommend that candidates ask for feedback. They are entitled to it, and it helps them for future interviews. If the company allows time to interpret results prior to a job offer or second interview, then they are using the test fully as part of the hiring decision making process. Candidates should expect to be asked questions about their behaviour or work preferences in subsequent interviews.

How important are the results of a test?

As companies invest money in administering tests and assessing results, they value the results highly. The test results form an important part of building an understanding of the individual's capabilities. An interview will either support or counter psychometric results. It is the right overlap between personal characteristics, behaviour, and knowledge and experience that an interviewer is interested in (see Figure 1.2 in Chapter 1). An individual may make up in personality or attitude for what he or she lacks in knowledge or experience. Ultimately it is for the interviewer to decide if the individual's mix of characteristics, knowledge and behaviour meets the requirements. The judgment is based on the interviewer's individual assessment of the candidate.

Can candidates cheat?

Yes, they can cheat in some tests, but some tests contain lie detectors, which means that inconsistent answers are highlighted in the test results. A recruiter will typically explore themes and trends that have come out of a psychometric test at interview. (See the box on page 149 for an interviewer's assessment guide.) It's important for the candidate to be realistic and honest. If a job that a candidate is applying for involves a lot of travelling, and the candidate lies and says that she enjoys travelling when she doesn't, she won't be happy in the role. She will probably end up leaving before her probationary period is finished, which is frustrating for her and for her employers.

What should candidates be looking out for when completing selection tests?

As I've already said, they should ask for feedback. Also most tests contain a very detailed job description, as they deal with competencies that are core to the role to be filled. You can also find out a lot about the openness of an organization, based on how much they tell you about how they treat the results. An open organization will send selection test feedback to all participating candidates. The decision to offer a candidate a job is almost exclusively dependent upon how well the recruiter, or recruiters, believe the candidate meets their requirements.

Sample interviewer's assessment guide

Interview summary points

When interviewing the sample person you should consider his personal characteristics in the context of the proposed role.

His low structural score suggests that you should consider the following:

Does the role require an organized approach? If so, how will he accommodate this requirement? Ask him to describe occasions when he has had to be particularly organized, and probe into how effective he was at this.

Discuss how he manages his workload in order to meet his commitments.

Does he find himself avoiding structure whenever he can?

How well will he work alongside more meticulous and organized colleagues?

His above average conformity score suggests that you should consider the following:

Will the absence of rules and procedures reduce his effectiveness?

Discuss whether he tends to experience problems when working with unconventional colleagues.

Evaluate how he reacts to changes introduced by others.

Does the role require him to have an innovative approach? If so, how effective will he be?

His relatively low confidence score suggests that you should consider the following:
Is he sufficiently decisive for the role?
Discuss how he manages stress and pressure.
Will he have an overly pessimistic approach to the challenges he will face?
Question him on how he handles criticism and whether he finds it particularly demotivating.

(Adapted from the PSL Rapid Personality Questionnaire Report)

Although you can practise ability tests and improve your scores, personality tests do not elicit right or wrong answers. The best advice is to be honest in your responses so that recruiters can make sound hiring decisions.

ASSESSMENT CENTRES

As you are by now well aware, 'chance favours the prepared mind'. You can prepare for assessment centres in much the same way as you would prepare for an interview or construct a targeted cover letter. Our starting point, as always, is company research (refer to Chapter 3). Through conducting this research you should be able to identify the recruiter's requirements and appraise yourself of industry news. This enables recognition of the challenges that the company may be facing, and also indicates how you could assist the company in achieving its objectives.

If you are due to be assessed for a job within a public sector organization as opposed to private industry, your preparation should differ slightly. Unless you already have a high level of general knowledge, you should develop it through either reading a daily national broadsheet for at least a fortnight prior to your assessment, or daily watching world and national news. Know who your appropriate minister is – for example, the Minister for Health if healthcare is your chosen profession – and be aware of recent legislative changes that may be affecting your sector. In addition public sector candidates should:

- ☐ practise entry level fitness tests, if applicable;
- ☐ be prepared to disclose their medical history, if applicable;
- ☐ rehearse practical scenarios, such as survival plans for a group lost in the desert (this type of role play is used in, for example, armed forces officer selection).

If you are due to be assessed for a senior position in private industry your assessment may consist of many of the public sector selection criteria. Additionally it is common practice to test candidates' leadership abilities and styles, decision making processes and problem solving abilities.

If you are set a hypothetical problem or critical situation to solve, practise structuring your answers in a logical, concise manner. If you are set a problem such as this in an exam situation, use bullet points, headings and diagrams in your answer. Aim to write a plan, rather than an essay, as your answer.

If the answer is spoken, tell your audience how you are going to answer the question before you start your answer. For example: 'I'm going to outline the pros and cons of this situation before I explain the action plan that will resolve it.' Typically people do not hear the first few seconds of a conversation. By introducing your answer, you should ensure that the interviewers are listening to you when you are explaining your solution. For a list of psychometric and ability test sites with descriptions and further reading on assessment tests, see Appendix 1.

ASSESSMENT CENTRE LOWDOWN

How Tesco uses assessment

Tesco UK (http://www.tesco.com) has recently developed an online competency questionnaire as a sifting tool for its graduate assessment centres. Kate Aspinwall is the Graduate Recruitment Manager for Tesco UK (http://www.tesco.com/graduates). In the interview below Kate describes the assessment centre process.

What career paths does Tesco recruit graduates into?

We have three forks of recruitment, which are:

☐ store management;
☐ specialist head office (HO) management;
☐ general management in disciplines such as commercial and marketing.

Our store management recruitment also incorporates store personnel roles, where the focus is on an HR career path within our stores. Managers are trained in-store for two years and are appointed to a senior team position at the end of this term, if they successfully qualify. Within five years they can expect to be promoted to store manager. Store personnel recruits pursue an HR development role, which culminates in regional personnel positions. Responsibilities include recruitment, training and development for all stores within the region.

Our specialist HO management recruitment is designed for roles such as finance and IT. Recruits spend three months in-store so that they get to know our core business. It's important for all of our staff to understand how what they do in their ultimate job impacts our stores. Specialist training is for one year except for the financial roles where training is for three years, as this incorporates the CIMA (Chartered Institute of Management Accountants) qualification. Specialist HO graduates manage small projects while training, progressing to larger projects on training completion.

Our general management programme is for graduates who will perform key business functions, such as HR, commercial and marketing, throughout the business. The training for these graduates lasts for 18 months, six months of which is spent in-store. These graduates develop essential management skills first, prior to developing more specialist business expertise skills. This programme is aimed at developing managers within HO who have transferable management skills.

How do competency tests fit into your graduate recruitment programmes?

We use competency tests throughout Tesco for internal promotional and lateral moves, and also at the recruitment stage. Competency tests are not reserved for graduates alone, they form part of our Human Resource Strategy at Tesco (see Figure 8.1). We recently developed an online graduate competency test with Psychometric Services Ltd (PSL). The test is the first sifting stage of our graduate recruitment programme. Successful applicants are invited to attend an interview and then, if successful, a one and a half day assessment programme.

Figure 8.1 *Tesco recruitment process and use of competency tests. This illustration is used for HR training purposes.*
Source: *courtesy of Tesco*

What does the online graduate screening test comprise of?

There are several sections to the test, and it is designed to measure the suitability of candidates to jobs and roles within Tesco. There are no right or wrong answers to the test because it's about matching candidates to jobs. As we are a major UK employer there are many variations of jobs and roles within our company.

The test is timed so that we can get a feel for a candidate's instinctive response to a question. For this type of a test a candidate's first answer is usually the most accurate one. We would advise candidates to read any test that they take carefully. People do have a tendency to skip-read online, which could produce inaccurate results. Candidates should aim to answer online test questions as correctly as they would if they were taking the test in exam conditions. (For a sample question with possible answers see the box.)

Sample question from Tesco online graduate screening test

Please rank how comfortable you are in the following activities:
1   Very comfortable
2   Quite comfortable
3   I don't mind but I don't necessarily enjoy it
4   Somewhat comfortable
5   Not very comfortable at all

1. Doing a lot of different things at the same time.
2. Making decisions without referring to others.
3. Working in an extremely commercial environment.
4. Motivating others to achieve a goal.
5. Making decisions that might adversely affect others.
6. Building rapport with new people.
7. Writing reports.
8. Working with numbers.
9. Coping with a heavy workload.
10. Living with constant change.
11. Negotiating with people.
12. Getting others to work harder.
13. Making rapid decisions.
14. Working through complex numerical calculations.
15. Making decisions on the basis of limited information.

(Supplied courtesy of Tesco)

What should candidates expect when they attend your graduate assessment centre?

The assessment intake is usually between 80 to 120 candidates. On the first day candidates visit a store or see a presentation on the business function they are hoping to be recruited into. In the evening they have dinner and stay overnight. The first day is about getting to know the candidates and putting them at their ease. It's also fairer on the candidates to have an opportunity to get to know the others in their group before they commence any group exercises. The candidates are not assessed at any point on the first day. The second day is a full day, where candidates are assessed on soft skills and also specific business functions that are relevant to the positions they have applied for. So the second day is a mix of practicals and exercises that assess candidates' capabilities with regard to business functions such as: marketing, finance and IT. We assess candidates' work preferences and how they behave in a group. Typically four assessors observe a group of eight candidates (see Figure 8.2). Each assessor is responsible for a maximum of two candidates, and these rotate for each exercise.

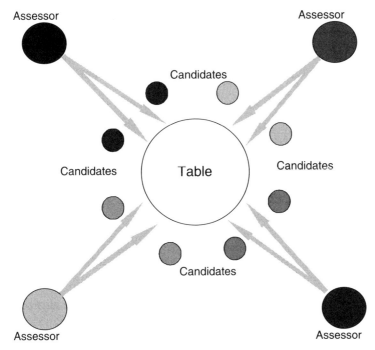

Figure 8.2   *Example of group exercise at Tesco assessment centre*
Source: Tesco

What do you watch out for when you are assessing candidates?

We are trained on assessing candidates' capabilities and behaviour. We score candidates on the behaviours that we are observing, and the scoring method is simple. For example in a team working exercise such as Tower Building, where candidates are tasked with jointly building a tower to specifications within a set time period, we monitor how individual candidates participate and contribute to the group using a behaviourally anchored rating scale (see Figure 8.3). We are not looking to recruit Superman and Superwoman, we want to recruit candidates who are the most suitable for the job.

TEAMWORKING

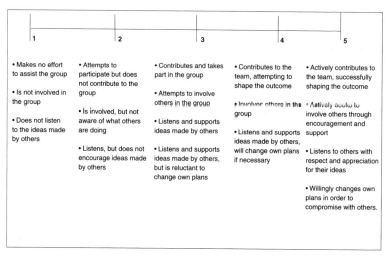

Figure 8.3 *Example of Tesco assessment centre teamwork exercise assessment*

What advice would you give to candidates who are due to attend an assessment centre?

We recommend that they prepare for the assessment centre. If they are applying for a specialist role in IT or finance they may be required to take ability tests. For example we test our finance candidates on their numeric ability. With regard to teamwork and management exercises, candidates should really just relax and be themselves. These sorts of behavioural tests are designed to let a person's preferences show through. Teams need to be balanced, and most companies favour diversity and recognize the importance of employing different personality types.

SUMMARY

We now know that selection tests are common, and we should be able to identify what we are likely to be assessed on. If you have been invited to attend a selection centre, remember that you have already passed the most difficult stage: you are one of the finalists. Through preparing carefully you should also be one of the winners.

9 Interview well

When the time comes for you to attend an interview, the extent of your research will escalate your chances of getting the job offer. The research tips that were given in Chapters 3 and 4 should provide you with the right answers to interview questions. Although your company research forms the foundation of your interview preparation, you should build role-specific information on top of it. These are the finer details, which answer queries about what the job will entail: how is the team structured? Who would I report to?

If team working, for example, is an integral part of the role, you should have thought of an example of a previous successful team working experience so that you can demonstrate your fit with this requirement. One way to discover more about the role is by calling the recruiter or hiring manager responsible for the vacancy, and asking him or her for a job description. If he or she is unable to provide a job description, you could ask the following questions:

- [ ] Is the work team or individually based?
- [ ] How many people are in the team?
- [ ] Who would I report to?
- [ ] In a typical week how much time is spent off site or in the office (role dependent)?
- [ ] Who are your biggest customers?
- [ ] Who are your competitors?
- [ ] Is there a dress code (role dependent – uniforms may be provided)?

From the job description or company research you should already understand how well the role would meet the ergonomic factors of your ideal working environment: whether it is in an open plan corporate office, call centre with booths, home office, factory, retail outlet, restaurant, hotel, gym, submarine, or is outdoor work, field work or whatever.

Another source of role-specific information is 'realistic job previews' such as video footage of the company and employees at work. If these are unavailable, try speaking to existing employees.

INTERVIEW TYPES

In Chapter 8 we explored selection tests for interview. This chapter examines the interview process and the different types of interviews that you may experience. It will also analyse interview purposes.

You may be interviewed by a panel (think *Pop Idol*) or an individual recruiter. The interview may be structured or unstructured. You may be asked to give a practical demonstration of your knowledge or expertise (for example, prepare a presentation for a customer) or solve a hypothetical problem on the spot. The purpose of this is to establish whether or not:

- [ ] you could do the job;
- [ ] you would do the job;
- [ ] you would fit in.

Recruitment interviews really are that simple. What complicates them are the following:

- [ ] inexperienced interviewers (it is estimated that less than 10 per cent of British managers are trained in interview techniques);
- [ ] ill prepared interviewees;
- [ ] nerves.

In order to help you get to grips with nerves and preparing for interviews, we have invited past master career manager Neil Lewis back to share his interview expertise.

Ask an expert

To briefly reintroduce Neil, he is the Managing Director of Working Careers, a career management company and wholly owned subsidiary of outplacement specialists Fairplace plc (http://www.workthingcareers.com

or http://www.fairplace.com). Working Careers provides CV writing, interview coaching and career management services to job seekers.

When should an interviewee expect a panel as opposed to a one to one interview?

Panel interviews most commonly occur in public sector organizations, and they may occur when candidates attend assessment days or weekends. For example the armed forces and emergency services frequently panel interview for internal promotions or lateral moves. They also frequently run assessment days or weekends for recruitment purposes. In general, as smaller organizations do not have a single expert recruiter, candidates may experience interviews being conducted by interested parties such as several prospective bosses within the organization.

If the role that the interviewee is applying for has a cross-departmental or cross-regional function, there may be more than one decision maker involved in choosing the right candidate. For example a business development manager may have targets set by a finance director, objectives set by a sales director and partnership strategy set by the managing director. All three stakeholders would have a say in deciding who was hired. If they were not directly involved in a panel interview they might each have a representative present during the interview.

Larger organizations, with personnel or HR departments, are more likely to employ expert interviewers, which means that they can staff one to one interviews. We would recommend that candidates prepare for both interview types, and find out from their prospective employer, if they can, who is going to be conducting the interview.

How does being interviewed by a panel change the way that an interviewee should answer questions?

The content and structure of the answers should still be the same, and answers should be kept short and to the point. But if an interviewee is answering a question from a panel member, he or she should direct the answer to the interviewer who posed the question, and make eye contact with him or her. We would recommend that even though an interviewee wants to influence the group, there is a danger in trying to make eye contact with the whole group. If one panel member is not paying attention when the candidate is answering a question, the interviewee might be put off, which would affect his or her performance on the day.

On a one to one basis, interviews are a lot easier. An interviewee should establish eye contact when he or she begins the answer, but it can distract people if constant eye contact is maintained. So the occasional break in eye contact is advisable.

What is the difference between structured and unstructured interviews?

In a structured interview the same questions are asked of each candidate. This is so that all the interviewees' answers can be compared and matched with the desirable answers.

Structured interviews are more common in larger organizations that have HR departments. If candidates have undergone screening or selection tests it is likely that they will have structured interviews. The interviewer will try to explore traits or abilities that have been uncovered in the test results. Usually structured interviews are favoured by professional recruiters or hiring managers.

In a structured interview candidates are only able to answer the questions that are put in front of them. Structured interviews are more testing for the candidate than unstructured interviews. Candidates may feel like they are having a difficult time, but this is likely to be every interviewee's experience. The advantage of structured interviews is that the interviewer is assisted in making an objective decision, because like for like comparisons can be made. In addition the feedback from structured interviews tends to be more comprehensive.

In many ways unstructured interviews are trickier for interviewees. Unstructured interviews can leave the interviewee confused as to what the job entails, or whether or not they will be made a job offer. Some interviewers deliberately use an unstructured interview style to elicit spontaneous responses, to get the interviewee to drop his or her guard. Unstructured styles may be utilized during interviews for creative roles in media and entertainment.

We would advise interviewees to make a list of questions that they want to be answered during the interview. In this way, regardless of the interview structure, they should know enough after an interview to be able to decide whether or not they should take the job offer if it is made.

When should an interviewee expect to be asked to give a practical or hypothetical demonstration of knowledge or expertise?

Almost certainly for a sales or customer service role, or as part of an assessment day or weekend. And public sector promotions or specialist career moves usually require candidates to sit a selection interview board. During these boards interviewees are asked hypothetical questions to test for knowledge of, for example, legislation, organizational policies, or health and safety issues.

If a candidate is asked either a hypothetical question or to perform a task, he or she should be sure of what has been asked before answering. It's better to confirm the question than risk blundering the response.

We would recommend that applicants for all roles prepare for this and practise different scenarios. This should mean that on the day, even if they are nervous, they should still perform well.

It is human nature to forget things and perform routine tasks like an amateur when under pressure. You've only got to watch a penalty shoot out to see the truth in this. Athletes can overcome the negative effects of stress through training and rehearsal. This approach works just as well for candidates. We would advise candidates to consider how they would perform different tasks before an interview, and to run through them with a friend, or better still a mentor. That way if they are asked to perform or hypothesize, their response should be a professional one that impresses the interviewer.

How does an interviewee demonstrate that he or she could do the job?

The employer's requirements are listed in the job description or person specification (which describes essential and desirable skills for a job). So if for example 'good communication skills' is specified in the job description, the candidate should prepare an example of how his or her good communication skills have won business, or saved the organization money or satisfied a customer in the past. Ideally an interviewee should be able to demonstrate that he or she has performed well in the past on similar tasks to those required to do the job.

If candidates don't have a job description they will have to rely on their own company research and knowledge about the role that they are applying for. In this case it is even more important to network effectively. Candidates should call their prospective boss, or employees who perform similar roles, to check what the job is like.

How do interviewees show that they would do the job?

By answering the interviewer's questions in such a way as to show that they have done their research and that they understand the interviewer's market. For example if the interviewer was to ask 'How would you deal with a customer complaint that their product was faulty?', an interviewee who had done his or her research might respond, 'I know you have a money back guarantee policy, so having checked the item and the customer's receipt, I would apologize for the inconvenience that they had been caused and offer them their money back.'

The interviewee has shown that he or she has thought about how he or she would behave if he or she were doing the job for which he or she is applying. This is probably as close to 'would do' as a candidate can get without actually being offered the job. It would be appropriate to ask questions about the company at this stage. The questions might explore company expansion plans, product development or policy changes. Again the interviewee is showing how he or she might contribute to the future development of the company.

How does an interviewee verify that he or she would fit in?

This is where the person specification research and networking really help. If interviewees do not know who they will be working with, or who they will be reporting to, they are unlikely to be able to guess what questions the interviewer may ask of them. However, if the interviewee knows that he or she would be working with a large team in an open plan office where it is desirable to have a good sense of humour, then he or she should expect a question about team work. He or she can then pitch the answer accordingly.

We would strongly advise interviewees to be honest about their work preferences. If they would not enjoy working in an environment like this, then they should say so. They would be better to spend their job hunting time on roles that would make them happier, where they should perform better.

This is also a good time for interviewees to ask any questions that they have prepared about their prospective boss, or colleagues, and any training that might be given if the job was offered.

After the job offer we would recommend that the interviewee asks to spend time with the team prior to commencing employment. This is the best way that candidates can verify that they fit in. And it's not too late to decline the job offer if the culture is not what was expected by the candidate.

INTERVIEW TIPS

What top tips would you give interviewees?

There are two main tips that we would give. The first is about preparation and the second is about self-belief. Preparation is everything, because if a candidate fails to prepare then the result may be that he or she fails. The preparation starts with company research and networking, and finishes with planning the journey to the interview and making sure that he or she turns up in clean shoes.

Interview practice is an important part of the preparation process. Candidates should aim to get as much interview practice as possible. They could consider going for interviews for jobs that they are not absolutely sold on, just to improve their interview techniques. We would still urge candidates to concentrate their job hunting efforts on jobs that fall within zone A of their zone of possibility (see Figure 9.1). But if a candidate hasn't had an interview in years, practice will quickly help to build their confidence.

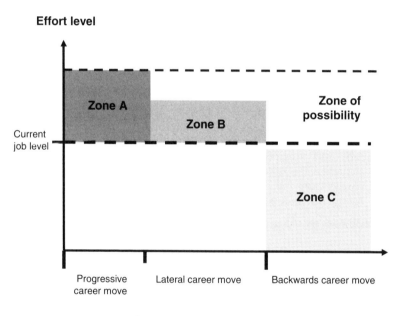

Figure 9.1 *Zones of possibility*

Our second tip is about self-belief. If a candidate has been invited to an interview, it means that the company is seriously considering hiring him or her, and that he or she is already halfway there. If the candidate is self-confident and prepared, there is no reason he or she should not be offered the job. It is important that candidates believe this, otherwise lack of self-belief and nerves on the day could be wrongly construed as incompetence. More specifically we would recommend that interviewees should:

- ☐ Arrive in good time for the interview about 10 minutes before.
- ☐ Be appropriately dressed.
- ☐ Shake hands in a firm, positive manner.
- ☐ Smile – it helps to relax the interviewee and interviewer.
- ☐ Sit down when invited and where indicated.
- ☐ Check his or her posture – avoid slouching.
- ☐ Try not to fidget and if he or she does gesticulate, keep hands at or below elbow level.
- ☐ Maintain good eye contact.
- ☐ Use interviewers' names if they are known. If an interviewer calls the candidate by his or her first name, it's OK for the interviewee to call the interviewer by his or hers in return.
- ☐ Listen carefully.
- ☐ Give clear, concise answers.
- ☐ Stress his or her suitability for the post by giving results-oriented examples of what he or she has achieved.
- ☐ Ask questions he or she has prepared when asked to do so. If the prepared questions have already been answered, he or she should tell the interviewers this.
- ☐ Always thank the interviewer or interviewers for their time.
- ☐ Always ask for feedback.

Interviewees should avoid:

- ☐ Smoking.
- ☐ Criticizing former employers or colleagues.
- ☐ Talking about their domestic circumstances unless specifically asked to do so.
- ☐ Bringing up the research that they have conducted on a company. It should be delivered in answer to the interviewer's questions.
- ☐ Bringing a portfolio or examples of their work, unless specifically asked to do so.
- ☐ Arguing.
- ☐ Being meek.
- ☐ Being boastful.
- ☐ Discussing salaries until a job offer has been made.

How should interviewees answer questions?

Their style should be open but discreet, and show enthusiasm. They should give the interviewer their full attention and avoid reading from their CV or taking notes. They should try to give real, specific examples, and be concise in what they say. If the question confuses them or they don't hear it, they should ask for clarification. This is much better than giving the wrong answer or answering a question with a question, which can appear confrontational.

If in answering a question there is an opportunity for the interviewee to talk about additional skills or areas of expertise, he or she should do so.

If candidates are asked negative questions, they should answer positively. For example the question might be, 'Why do you want to leave your current job?' The candidate might answer, 'I really enjoy my current job, but I have evolved beyond the role and as the company is small, I am unlikely to have the opportunity to develop further if I stay.' This is a much better response than 'The company's going nowhere and I want to get out before it's too late', even if the latter response is truer than the former.

Candidates should also spend more time talking about relevant and recent experience. This is particularly pertinent for career changers or for candidates who have reskilled to make a lateral career move.

INTERVIEW QUESTIONS AND ANSWERS

Can you give some examples of typical questions and ideal responses?

Recruitment interview questions fall into five general groups. The first group consists of opening questions that are designed to get candidates talking and to put them at their ease. Some examples of opening questions are:

☐ Tell me about yourself.
☐ Could you summarize your career?
☐ Describe the last three jobs that you have had.

The interviewer is looking for candidates to verbalize their profile statements. Candidates should aim to talk for about 30 to 45 seconds, and mention five or six items only. They could discuss skills, strengths, achievements, job roles, work experiences, their qualifications and obstacles that they have overcome. The purpose of their response should be to demonstrate to the interviewer that they have the right mix of characteristics, knowledge and experience to do the job.

The second group are 'can do it' questions. These questions test an interviewee's abilities, knowledge, experience, personal characteristics and predisposition to do the job. Answers to 'can do it' questions should be results-led, and are like a spoken version of achievements as listed on a CV. Examples of common 'can do it' questions are:

☐ *What are your strengths?* If an interviewer asks about strengths, he or she is asking the interviewee about his or her personal attributes, what he or she is naturally good at. It may be that the candidate is sociable and approachable. This could be cited as a rapport building strength, which would be an appropriate attribute for a sales job. Interviewees should list up to three strengths relevant to the job description.

☐ *What would you bring to our company if you were to work for us?* The answer to this question is a great opportunity for candidates to tell interviewers not just how they could do the job, but how they could do the job better than anyone else. The interviewee should give one example of a previous work experience that was successful and is closely related to the job that he or she is being interviewed for. Again the response should focus on results. The interviewee could talk about increased turnover, reduced cost or happy customers.

☐ *What have been the two most significant achievements in your career?* This is another opportunity question, where a targeted response will verify for the interviewer that the candidate can do the job. The response should be analogous with the role.

The third question type is 'will do it' questions. These questions explore whether or not a candidate will do the job if he or she is given the position. A recruiter is seeking to identify the candidate who will hit the ground running by asking 'will do it' questions. Examples of 'will do it' questions are:

☐ *What motivates you?* Ideally the interviewee's answer should describe work preferences that match those of the job. If the role is a self-starter one, where the employee is expected to work alone and rely on his or her own initiative, that is the answer candidates should give to the recruiter.

☐ *Where do you want to be in five years' time?* What the interviewer is asking here is, 'Are your ambitions aligned with the role, or the company's future?' They want to qualify that the candidate will not only do the job, but will do it for more than one month. They want to confirm that the candidate will stay motivated by the role and the company. When answering this question the candidate should give an example of a future role that is an evolved version of the job he or she is applying for. This isn't as difficult as it sounds. If the candidate is applying for a sales manager role he or she could say that his or her ambition is to be a sales director, or a sales team trainer, or an expert in the field of 'widget' consultancy sales.

☐ *Why do you want this job?* In answering this question candidates have an opportunity to link their answer to their company research. The interviewer wants to test how interested the interviewee is in the job. So based on the candidate's research, he or she might answer, 'I want to be given the opportunity to take your latest widget to market. I know that it is more competitively priced than Company B's or C's and is a far superior product.' The candidate has shown that he or she knows about a new product and the company's main competitors. He or she has already visualized how he or she would market or sell the company's product.

The fourth category of questions is 'will you fit in' questions. Obviously the purpose of these questions is to verify that recruits would work with and not against their prospective team and boss. Some examples of 'will you fit in' questions are:

☐ *How would your colleagues describe you?* Candidates should answer this within the context of work. Any references to extra-work activity might prejudice the outcome of the interview. A good response might be 'Loyal, supportive, calm in a crisis and helpful'. This is more of a personality traits question than anything else. So once again candidates should talk about their personal assets, what they are naturally good at.

☐ *How would you describe your work style?* This is a question about your work preferences. It is better if candidates tailor their answer to the type of working environment they expect to perform the role in. If the majority of the work is as part of a team, the candidate should give an example of how he or she successfully accomplished a task as part of a team.

☐ *How did you get on with your last manager?* The answer to this question can really only ever be 'Very well'. Candidates should endeavour to highlight the positive aspects of their working relationship with their boss. For example, if they disagreed on occasion with their boss this could be paraphrased as 'an open relationship where constructive criticism and free thought were encouraged'.

The last type of questions is nasty questions. These are structured in such a way as to catch candidates out and put them on the spot, so it really helps if interviewees have already practised answering them. Candidates shouldn't be thrown by nasty questions – they are just as much an opportunity to shine as nicer, more predictable questions. Nasty questions may be asked during a structured interview as part of test results analysis probing. Interviewers may be validating the traits and trends that have been shown in competency test results, so candidates should not be afraid of them. Common examples of nasty questions include:

☐ *How do you deal with stress?* Candidates should remember that stress is not the same as pressure, and might answer, 'I deal with any pressurized situations at work as they arise. Usually I have some spare time to deal with unpredictable events because I manage my time so as to meet deadlines ahead of schedule.' Candidates should also emphasize their ability to neutralize stress through relaxing when away from work. They could describe out of work activities. The key to answering this question well is to reassure the interviewer that work is efficiently managed at work, during work time.

☐ *What would you say are your weaknesses?* Candidates can answer this question and turn it to their advantage. What they should actually do is talk about a strength. For example, 'I'm so passionate about my work, that if I thought something was a bad idea I would tell the person concerned why I thought it was a bad idea, even if they were my boss.' What the interviewee has actually said is that he or she is courageous, open, honest, and takes the business objectives to heart.

☐ *Why were you made redundant?* Redundancy is now a common occurrence, and there is no stigma attached to it. If a recruiter asks this question it is probably because he or she wants to ensure that the interviewee was not made redundant for any negative reasons. A response might be, 'The redundancy resulted from a company wide reorganization. It is unfortunate that my position was deleted. However, it has given me the opportunity to look for new challenges, and I am very much looking forward to that.'

When should candidates discuss salaries and benefits?

It is far better if the interviewer raises the matter first. We would advise that if the candidate raises it too early in the process it could seem like he or she is more interested in the money than the job. The best time to negotiate is when the candidate is absolutely sure that he or she will be offered the job. Candidates shouldn't wait until the offer is in writing, because it's far more difficult to negotiate the package when it has got to the employment contract stage.

How can candidates find out what sort of salary they should expect?

Some salaries, mainly public sector, are published in year books (found in the business reference sections of libraries) and also on government or corporate sites. In addition salary survey results can be found in the reference sections of libraries. Workthing has a Salary Checker on its site, which calculates salaries based on the role and location of the job in question (http://www.Workthing.com/servlet/salarysurveyinput). To get an idea of market rate salaries, candidates should collate job advertisements for the role or roles for which they are applying.

How should candidates negotiate their salaries?

Before they start negotiating they need to work out the total value of their package before and after tax. Tax calculations become more pressing if the salary would put the candidate just into a higher rate tax threshold. In some cases candidates might be better off earning a smaller wage with more non-taxable benefits. Packages should be calculated with benefits such as pensions, bonuses, cars, private healthcare, share options, personal development grants, training grants and travel expenses all included. Once the candidate has decided on a salary, he or she should be prepared to give the prospective employer a realistic salary range. If the package is lower than the candidate's expectations, he or she should try to negotiate rather than reject the offer. We would recommend that candidates:

☐ Start by stating the range of the salary that they want and then move to the benefits package.
☐ Back up their 'asking price' with a rationale to support their position. The rationale could be their researched salary market figures and their commitment to the job.
☐ If prospective employers refuse to negotiate, candidates should ask for more time to consider the offer.
☐ If a candidate knows at this stage that he or she is going to refuse the job offer, he or she should endeavour to end the discussion on a pleasant note, so that the company would still consider him or her for any future, more suitable openings.

SUMMARY

Candidates should defend their worth and the value of what their placement would bring to the organization. We would advocate that all of these actions are symbolic of a job seeker who carefully evaluates a situation before making a decision. Regardless of the job that the candidate is applying for, a businesslike approach is an attribute that will be recognized and valued by a prospective employer.

Chapters 1 to 9 should have equipped you with an expert's insight into:

- ☐ finding your happy work reality;
- ☐ identifying your ideal working environment mix;
- ☐ masterminding your next career move;
- ☐ knowing your employability worth;
- ☐ developing Olympian job hunting techniques;
- ☐ making the right first impression;
- ☐ writing winning CVs;
- ☐ polishing your performance;
- ☐ interviewing well.

Although this is an enviable framework for making the right career moves, you may have some questions that are unique to your job search that have not been answered. The next chapter deals with troubleshooting, and features your corner, where unusual but nonetheless frequent candidate questions are posed and answered.

10 | Trouble-shooting

The Right Career Moves Handbook is full of ideas and expert opinions that will hopefully send you on your way to your happy work reality. It is an actuality for some, however, that seemingly insurmountable obstacles may turn career dreams to vapour. In this chapter we recognize some common problems and job hunting frustrations, and suggest ways to overcome them.

CANDIDATES' CORNER

Career expert

We can welcome Neil Lewis back from Working Careers (http://www.workthingcareers.com), and repeat his advice on a number of issues that candidates may face.

If candidates' CVs are not getting them shortlisted, how can they change this?

In most cases if a CV is not getting a candidate shortlisted it's because it is not targeted enough. It's a bit like waiting on the wrong platform for a train. Candidates can improve their CVs by:

- ☐ targeting their CV to the job;
- ☐ highlighting their relevant skills, experience and achievements;
- ☐ adding an effective personal profile;
- ☐ including only information that is relevant to the job – recruiters don't like 'Jacks of all trades';
- ☐ keeping their CV to two pages.

We would recommend that if a candidate is already a little dispirited because he or she has not been shortlisted, he or she get a second opinion from an expert.

The government has recently illuminated the plight of middle-aged job seekers. How can candidates overcome ageism?

We would advise more mature candidates to leverage off their existing network when job hunting. A speculative approach to job hunting should serve to reduce the number of young competitors for the same positions, whereas responses to advertised jobs are likely to attract high numbers of responses from younger candidates.

The principles of job hunting are the same regardless of age, so candidates should focus on what they can do. Mature candidates are advantaged because they are experienced employees, and experience is a valuable commodity for businesses.

We recommend that candidates choose energetic hobbies when they list their interests on their CV. In an interview situation candidates should be proud of their age, not defensive. We provide information regarding age-friendly employers and career management services specifically for the over-50s (http://www.workthingcareers.com). In addition, candidates could visit community sites where career management services and the latest updates on ageism policies are listed (http://www.over50s.com or http://www.fifthmoon.com).

How can candidates ask if they've got the job without sounding pushy?

We would recommend that they don't ask because it won't make a difference anyway. If a candidate feels he or she has to ask because he or she has another job offer, then this is best explained to the interviewer after the interview.

If a candidate thinks he or she is going to be offered more than one job, how can he or she pick one without burning any bridges?

First, candidates should try to synchronize the job offers, so they can make a decision knowing all the facts. One way to achieve this would be to call the interviewers and explain their predicament. Candidates should be careful of not sounding conceited, but should also explain that they want to make a full commitment to whichever organization they choose, and that they are unable to do this unless they know what is on offer.

When rejecting job offers candidates should be honest, but not brutal, with the recruiter. If they are choosing one job over another because of a preferential benefits package, there is no harm in saying this. They should aim to make the rejected party feel like the runners up, not the losers. It would be prudent, for example, to cite less travelling time or flexible working hours as deciding it, rather than better promotional prospects.

When is it appropriate to talk salaries?

When a candidate has a job offer. This is the time when his or her bargaining power is at its strongest.

If a candidate is in a job that pays well, but doesn't enjoy it, how can he or she career change and still pay the bills?

It does depend on the career change, but if individuals need to retrain they could look at devoting leisure time to furthering their education. If they need to gain experience then they could investigate doing a second job in their free time. Whatever they decide, they need to plan carefully and budget for a downturn in income. We work with a number of IFAs (independent financial advisors), and if the candidate feels it is appropriate we can make a referral. There is a lot to think about when career changing, and we would advise any candidate who is unsure of the financial risks involved to seek professional assistance.

If a candidate is pregnant and attending a job interview, should she tell her prospective boss?

Legally there is no obligation to do so. It really would be up to the candidate.

If a candidate had left his or her last job on bad terms, how should he or she answer a question about that in interview?

We would recommend that he or she keeps the answer short and positive. It's OK to edit answers, but candidates shouldn't lie. For example if the 'bad terms' were caused by a personality clash, this could be described as a difference in communicative styles.

If a candidate has rehearsed his or her interview technique and is still failing at interview, what might the cause be?

The first point to make is that it may not be the person's fault. It may simply be the case that he or she is competing against other candidates who match the recruiter's requirements better. One way of improving interview effectiveness is to video a mock interview. It may be that the candidate's body language is giving off the wrong signals. Assuming that he or she has prepared and researched for the interview, we would recommend that he or she videos a mock interview with a friend. Seeing yourself on film and hearing how you sound when you answer questions can be hugely valuable. Candidates should then be able to modify their behaviour so that how they seem in an interview is a fairer representation of who they are. We practise this as part of our face to face consultations, if candidates want help with their interview style. The feedback from candidates has been that this approach was more beneficial than using an image consultant, for example, because they were able to see for themselves how they could improve their posture, mannerisms or appearance for the purpose of gaining a job offer.

Some candidates who return to work after a long career break may fear that they will not be taken seriously. How can they convince prospective employers that they are serious about work?

They should stress the positive reasons for the break, and talk about what they gained from it. By keeping up to date with industry news and changes they should demonstrate that they have continued to evolve. Some public sector organizations insist that career break employees keep up to date with legislative and policy changes. A similar approach to private industry should convince prospective employers. Also candidates should state why they want to return to work, and in particular, why they want to work for the organization in question.

Some candidates may be rejected by prospective employers for being overqualified. Should they leave qualifications off their CVs?

We would advise candidates to first ask why they feel that they are overqualified. If they are being told this at interview, and prospective employers are expressing concerns about a candidate's commitment, it may be that the candidate is applying for zone C jobs and not zone A jobs. If the CV is tailored to the job then the candidate should not appear to be overqualified. Once again we would advise candidates not to lie. They may get caught out if their CV is screened, and spoil the prospect of any future job opportunities with the employer.

If a candidate has changed jobs frequently in a short period of time, how can he or she satisfy recruiters that he or she would stay in the new job?

It is advisable for the candidate to produce a functional or skill-led CV rather than a chronological one. He or she should also ask him or herself if he or she really does plan to stay. The person may want to reflect on why he or she changed jobs so often in the past, and perhaps avoid the same circumstances again. He or she should stress positive reasons for moving on to prospective employers.

Some candidates who have worked for the same company for many years may be concerned that recruiters will think they're dinosaurs. How can they allay the recruiters' concerns?

These candidates are likely to have gained skills and experience in the same organization. This should be stressed to employers. If the candidate has made lateral moves, been promoted or performed different jobs, these equal moving on. The different roles within the same organization can be referred to as separate jobs in the 'work history' part of the CV. Each role should be taken on its individual merits. Candidates should explain why they want the new job, as they would for any other career move.

Where can disabled candidates find jobs?

There are two sites that we would recommend candidates visit: U-can-do-it (http://www.ucandoit.org.uk), which carries a list of, and links to, useful sites for the disabled, and Opportunities (http://www.opportunities.org.uk), which features employers of choice for the disabled such as Procter and Gamble, the BBC, GlaxoSmithKline, and the Foreign and Commonwealth Office. In addition there are several government programmes available to the disabled. Work Preparation is a programme designed to help people back to work after a long period of unemployment caused by ill health or disability. Access to Work is a support programme for both the employer and the employee. The scheme can help to fund special equipment or a communicator for individuals with hearing impairments. These programmes can be accessed via the Opportunities site or via local employment offices.

What advice would you give to people who want to work abroad?

One of the safest ways to do this is to relocate within a large corporate employer, if such opportunities exist within the company. If this is not an option, we would recommend the individual researches the employment market of the country he or she hopes to move to. Information can be sourced via a reference library or the Internet. We would recommend visiting Going Global (http://www.goinglobal.com). This site specializes in country-specific PDF books (priced from $9.95 to $14.95 each, covering 75 countries), which contain details of employment trends, work permits and visas, local job sites, and CV format, interview and cultural advice.

Candidates need to consider different CV preferences. For example in mainland Europe most recruiters require candidates to attach a photograph to their CV. Identification cards, like our UK driving licences, are common in Europe, and photographs are widely used for identification purposes. CVs and cover letters in the United States are written differently from UK CVs. They tend to be more assertive and assumptive.

Employee rights, trade union powers and legislation vary greatly from country to country, so this is another area of research to consider. Individuals are also advised to work out their cost of living and factor in free UK services such as healthcare. These free services may not be provided by the state in destination countries.

People who carry out contract work abroad may qualify for UK tax breaks. We recommend that they seek advice from a tax accountant. Some recruitment consultancies that specialize in overseas contract work refer their candidates to preferred tax accountants.

FUND YOUR DREAM CAREER

Advice on financial advisers

Gary Elliot is the Managing Director of AdviceOnline (http://www.adviceonline.co.uk), a company that specializes in delivering the very latest independent financial advice and news to UK residents online. Users of AdviceOnline can compare and buy financial products, access product guides and explanations, search for a local accredited IFA, use interactive financial calculating tools, and link to world market and financial news. AdviceOnline is regulated by the Financial Services Authority (FSA).

What sort of help and advice could an IFA give to career movers?

As most people earn, rather than inherit, their income in the UK, IFAs are well placed to advise any candidate on the financial implications of their career move.

How do you choose an IFA?

You can either do an Internet search or look through a local directory for an IFA. We recommend that where possible, people choose one that is local, for convenience's sake. They should ensure that their IFA has a Financial Planning Certificate (FPC). This is the minimum qualification that an IFA should have. A competent adviser must hold all three components of this certificate or the equivalent. Some advisers also have advanced level qualifications in their specialist areas: for example, an Advanced Financial Planning Certificate for Pensions or Personal Investment Planning. Individuals may want to check:

☐ Who they are regulated by. An IFA should be regulated by a recognized authority. This is usually the FSA, which is the principal regulator for financial services.

☐ How long the IFA has been in business. They may feel more comfortable with someone who has several years' experience.

☐ What qualifications the IFA has: this should be at least the FPC, as described above.

☐ If they are specialists. Most IFAs are all-rounders but some specialize in mortgages, pension transfers, life assurance, accident and liability cover and the like.

☐ How they charge, which could be either fee or commission based. If an IFA works on a fees basis, this means the client is expected to pay a fee for the work he or she carries out. The amount is calculated and jointly agreed before any work commences. Alternatively the IFA might earn commission from the companies that provide the financial products the client purchases. The amount of commission should be disclosed to the client before he or she agrees to accept any of the products or services. Often commission can be used to offset any fees due.

Since an IFA works on the client's behalf, it's important that individuals establish a good working relationship with their IFA.

Some people feel they cannot change careers because of the financial risks. What advice would you give to them?

You should realistically assess the costs of the change by looking at:

☐ potential loss of income;
☐ costs associated with the change, such as fees, expenses and relocation costs;
☐ ongoing living expenses and fixed costs such as a mortgage, car and other loans, credit/store card payments and utility bills.

Add all of these up to assess the total expenditure, then show the total expenditure either as a one-off cost or as a cost spread over the duration of any education or training period. (For example, divide up the total expenditure into a monthly cost.) Check that any costs associated with ongoing or future training, professional membership subscriptions and so on will be covered by the likely salary, or factor these in as expenditure also. Then ask yourself if you have sufficient funds to cover this. If there is a financial shortfall you will need to investigate options to cover it. These might include:

☐ Student loans.
☐ Realistic remortgaging. You need to ensure that all payments can be covered in addition to other living expenses.
☐ Cutting and reducing expenditure to decrease the shortfall. This might involve relocating, changing or selling your car, amalgamating loans or debt consolidation.

The risk and cost of career changes should not only be quantified in terms of cost alone. Future career progression, increased earnings potential, personal development and job stability, as well as emotional happiness, are important factors that for many people could outweigh the financial costs or risks associated with career changing.

What advice would you give to students with regard to funding their education?

Plan in advance wherever possible. They should make sure they have the funds available to meet the realistic costs of their education. They should take measures to reduce costs if their funding is insufficient. Also they should investigate all loans and support options, such as:

☐ Grants and bursaries, including access bursaries to help with child care costs.
☐ Career development loans.

_____

- ☐ Scholarships may be an option.
- ☐ Find out if parents, grandparents or guardians have planned any provision that may help. Students may be able to access or cash in a wedding fund, or use parents' or guardians' equity.
- ☐ Or just ask and hope for a generous disposition.

What advice would you give to graduates and students with regard to reducing post qualification debts?

Most people rely on student loans to help fund their studies. Repayment of these loans happens automatically when income exceeds £10,000 a year. People should bear in mind that the interest rate on student loans is usually lower than for other forms of debt: for example in September 2002 it was set at 1.3 per cent. We would advise early repayment only where the individual has surplus cash, sufficient savings and emergency funds. We advise against dipping into emergency funds that could prevent a candidate from having to borrow through another route, such as personal loans, overdrafts or credit cards. Where loans are sourced through another route, individuals should pay off any at uncompetitive rates of interest as quickly as possible, but beware of any early repayment penalties.

What advice would you give to people re-entering the employment market after a career break?

They should carefully assess the package and deal offered by the new employer. Most people very quickly become accustomed to spending what they earn, or living within their means. They upgrade their car or clothes, go on expensive holidays and absorb any extra income. So the best time for them to seek financial advice is before they get used to spending their newly acquired income.

What advice would you give those considering working for themselves?

First, this covers two types of work: freelance or contract work, and entre-preneurial work, where people start their own businesses. If someone is considering freelancing, we would strongly advise him or her to get a good tax accountant early on. Much like career changers, freelancers need to work out their living expenses and be sure that possibly sporadic contracts will cover these fixed costs. Freelancers and contractors should also remember that companies provide benefits such as holiday pay, sick pay, company pensions, healthcare and personal development packages. If people choose to work for themselves, they will have to fund similar benefits from their own income.

Individuals thinking of starting their own business will probably need some help with a business plan. We recommend that they visit Business Link (http://www.businesslink.org), a government-run site that contains lots of information on starting and running your own business, and tips on grants and funding. An IFA could advise them on how to invest their income, but business owners need an accountant to advise them on their business accounting. We recommend that they shop around for their business banking provider, and do not just use their personal banking provider. Banking rates, packages and offers vary greatly, so they should place their business account with the provider that best suits their business needs. Most high street banks have an area on their sites dedicated to business banking, and it is possible to pick up free information and advice there.

PRE-EMPLOYMENT SCREENING

If you work in a position of trust or great responsibility with children or vulnerable persons, large amounts of money or sensitive information, your employers are legally bound to verify your history. Prospective employers may make a range of checks, depending on the role that you are applying for. Most employers outsource employee verification to professional agencies. There is some confusion over employee and employer rights with regard to these matters. We spoke to risk assessors Control Risks to find out more.

Advice from a risk assessor

Control Risks Group (http://www.crg.com) is an international business risk consultancy that offers a range of integrated political risk, investigative, security and crisis management services worldwide. Control Risks' pre-employment screening division is based in London, and is managed by Joanna Buckingham.

What sorts of companies use your services?

A range of companies in diverse sectors use our pre-employment screening services, including financial services, pharmaceuticals, food and drink, jewellers, petrochemicals, technology and charities.

Why do they use your services?

Companies use our services as an integral part of their recruitment processes. Pre-employment screening helps them minimize the risks of recruiting the wrong person, and in doing so helps them protect their brand and reputation. Control Risks builds a picture of an individual's integrity, confirming the facts provided by candidates about their academic and employment history, and their professional qualifications. We take up references and conduct various other checks such as residency and credit, media, and in some cases criminal records.

If proper checks are not undertaken, companies risk recruiting under-qualified individuals (who have misrepresented their qualifications), or those whose skills do not meet the requirements of the role (because individuals have exaggerated their employment history), or those who have a propensity for dishonesty or are untrustworthy.

In addition there have been legislative changes, which stipulate that for certain roles pre-employment screening is mandatory. Further to this, if checks are not carried out, the employer, employee or in some cases the employment agency (if one was used) is liable to be fined or prosecuted for any misdemeanours that occur as a result of employment.

For example in accordance with the Rehabilitation of Offenders Act (ROA) 1974 and (Exceptions) Order 1975, individuals within strict job categories such as finance managers, medical staff, teachers and individuals working with children and vulnerable adults undergo criminal record checks before they are employed. In order to facilitate pre-employment screening, the criminal records of individuals within strict job categories became available to prospective employers through the Criminal Records Bureau (CRB) in 2002. The CRB is an executive agency of the Home Office, and was set up to help organizations make safer recruitment decisions. By providing wider access to criminal record information, the CRB helps employers in the public, private and voluntary sectors identify candidates who may be unsuitable for certain work. Control Risks is a registered umbrella body, and liaises with the CRB in obtaining 'disclosure' of individuals' criminal records on behalf of prospective employers.

The advent of the Financial Services and Markets Act (2000) in December 2001 means that financial services companies are required to undertake due and diligent enquiries into the backgrounds of individuals within specific roles, and a robust pre-employment screening programme helps them meet this requirement. The Financial Services Authority (FSA) will regulate mortgage advice and the sale of general insurance products with effect from October 2004, and as a result, these industries will also have to undertake similar due and diligent enquiries.

Draft Regulations have been laid before Parliament under section 12(5) of the Employment Agencies Act 1973 (The Conduct of Employment Agencies and Employment Businesses Regulation). The new legislation will apply to workers who are employees of an employment or recruitment agency that provides staff to businesses.

Control Risks undertakes checks that are directly relevant to the role that is vacant. Specific skills may be required for a job. In this case, Control Risks will verify that candidates have the qualifications they claim to have, and back this up with a detailed check on an individual's employment history. We receive a brief from the prospective employer, which specifies the minimum requirements for the role in question. Armed with detailed knowledge about an individual, the prospective employer can take an informed decision as to whether or not the individual is the right person for the job.

What sorts of checks can employers make?

A number of standard checks are undertaken to confirm the facts provided by the candidate. These facts are usually provided in the application form. According to the Data Protection Act 1998 (DPA), employers are justified in taking steps to verify information provided by candidates, but prospective employers should use risk analysis as a tool for determining the amount of information required about a candidate. Information sought about an individual must be proportionate to the level of risk associated with the role. It is important that prospective employers only request relevant information. For example a prospective employer does not need to check whether a candidate has any driving offences if he or she is going to be working on a checkout. They would be advised, however, to check if the candidate has previous convictions for theft or other dishonesty-related offences. The essence of the DPA is transparency, so it is also important to tell candidates what is going to happen to their data.

Can candidates access the information themselves?

Yes. In accordance with the DPA, a candidate can apply in writing to see a copy of his or her pre-employment screening report. Candidates should apply to their prospective employer. A fee of £10 is payable, and the application can take up to 40 days to be processed.

If you discover an inconsistency in a CV, what do you do about it?

We go back to the candidate and double-check that he or she has not made an error. Control Risks can do this on a client's behalf, or the client (the prospective employer) may choose to do this. If it transpires that the candidate is lying, it is a question of judgement for the client as to whether or not the candidate is suitable for employment.

There may also be legal implications. For example, as far as the Financial Services Authority is concerned, under its Approved Persons regime, an individual with a County Court Judgement (CCJ) can still become an Approved Person, but only if he or she has disclosed the CCJ. If he or she has attempted to cover up the CCJ, their approval is negated.

What would your advice be to candidates with regard to the information on their CVs?

Do:

☐ be honest and accurate;
☐ provide a full academic and employment history;
☐ explain any gaps – travel, gap year, casual work, unemployment or whatever.

Don't:

☐ exaggerate your qualifications;
☐ try to cover up gaps between employment by 'extending' your employment dates;
☐ inflate your job title(s) or your salary.

CONCLUSION

Whether you have dipped into *The Right Career Moves Handbook* or read all of it, you should have broadened your job hunting knowledge and thus widened your job opportunities net. Remember to focus on what makes you happy and go after zone A jobs. Expect to find that your happy work reality changes as you progress through your career. Revisit your career plan, recall your achievements, and review it in line with your happy work realities. If you stay inspired and stick to your plan, career success will be yours.

Appendix 1: Resources

BIBLIOGRAPHY

Al-Jajjoka, S (2001) *How to Pass Professional Level Psychometric Tests*, Kogan Page, London. By providing plenty of practice material, this book aims to increase candidates' understanding of the types of tests they may face. Familiarity with these and the whole procedure has the added benefit of reducing nerves.

Barrett, J and Williams, T (2003) *Test Your Own Aptitude*, Kogan Page, London. From verbal reasoning to acuity skills, this book has every ability test (and answer) that a candidate might encounter. It ends with a complete index of over 400 roles in which aptitudes and personality traits are matched to careers.

Beatty, R H (1996) *The Perfect Cover Letter*, John Wiley, Hoboken, NJ. Written for the American market and full of examples of winning cover letters. The author advocates that a cover letter can showcase thinking abilities, writing skills and personality traits in a way that a CV cannot.

Bevan, J (2002) *The Rise and Fall of Marks and Spencer*, Profile Books, London. Marks and Spencer was one of Britain's most successful retailers. This chronicle of its history from the 1980s to the end of the 20th century seeks to explain why decline gripped the company.

Bishop-Firth, R (2002) *High Powered CVs: Powerful application strategies to get you that senior level job*, Essentials, London. Aimed at managers and professionals who want to stand out from the competition.

Bolles, R (2003) *What Colour is Your Parachute?*, Ten Speed Press, Berkeley, CA.

Brown, M (1989) *Richard Branson: The authorized biography*, Headline, London. Branson's biography is a roller coaster entrepreneurial success story. It guides the reader through the peaks and troughs of the Branson empire.

Catt, H and Scudamore, P (2000) *30 Minutes to Improve Your Networking Skills*, Kogan Page, London. This practical handbook demonstrates how everyone can build up their networks to gain more business, change jobs, attract new customers or get promoted.

Faust, B (2002) *Pitch Yourself*, Financial Times, Prentice Hall, London.

Fisher, D (1995) *People Power*, Cambridge Interactive Publications, Cambridge, MA. Provides a 12-stepped process to building and maintaining networks. Demystifies networking for the reader.

Fisher, D (2002) *Professional Networking for Dummies*, Wiley, Hoboken, NJ. As the title suggests, simplifies networking. The reader's attention is drawn to common networking mistakes so that they can be avoided.

Freer, I (2001) *The Complete Spielberg*, Virgin Books, London. A guide to all of Spielberg's projects whether successful or otherwise. A useful tool for any manager that works in media or entertainment.

Hermance, M, Fisher, D and Vilas, S (2000) *Power Networking: 59 secrets for personal and professional success*, Bard Press, New York. Full of useful tips on how to improve networking skills. Recommended as an indispensable tool for business professionals.

Kroc, R (1990) *Grinding It Out: The making of McDonald's*, St. Martin's Press, New York. From the first restaurant in Illinois to international franchise, Ray Kroc, the founder of McDonald's, tells the McDonald's story.

Malmsten, E (2002) *Boo Hoo: A dot com story*, Random House Business Books, London. *Boo Hoo* recounts the boom and bust of boo.com, an online clothing retailer. The story is told by its former founder and CEO. This is a useful insight into the importance of managing costs.

Nierenberg, A R (2002) *Non Stop Networking: How to improve your life, luck and career*, Capital Books, VA. This book advocates networking as a way of life. It is full of strategies for networking improvement with obvious benefits to the reader.

Perkins, G (2000) *Killer CVs and Hidden Approaches: Give yourself an unfair advantage in the executive job market*, Financial Times, Prentice Hall, London. This book is set to give executives an unfair advantage by giving an insight into the recruitment process from both sides.

Podesta, S and Paxton, A (2003) *201 Killer Cover Letters*, McGraw Hill Education, Columbus, OH. This book in disc format provides templates for appropriate cover letters. Models are provided for speculative (company and search and selection), advertisement response, networking and many more.

Roddick, A (2000) *Business as Unusual*, HarperCollins, London. Roddick details the progress of alternative cosmetics retailer The Body Shop. From the 1970s to the troubled 1990s, she shows the reader how she held on to her vision in the face of steep competition and negative press attention.

Stein, S and Book, H (2001) *The EQ Edge: Emotional intelligence and your success*, Kogan Page, London. Takes the mystery out of emotional intelligence. It's packed with case studies which demonstrate that emotional intelligence equals success. Readers can learn how to enhance EQ skills including problem solving and optimism.

Wallace, J (1997) *Overdrive: Bill Gates and the race to control cyberspace*, Wiley, Chichester. This collection of interviews with existing and former Microsoft employees, friends and competitors of Gates gives an insight into how Gates dealt with the new challenge of amassing Internet market share.

Welch, J (2001) *Jack: What I've learned leading great people and a great company*, Headline, London. As the title suggests this book demonstrates how Welch used his leadership style to transform GE in tandem with changing business practices.

Williams, L (2000) *Readymade CVs*, Kogan Page, London. This practical guide sets out the ground rules for preparing a CV by showing you how to select which details go in and which stay out.

Williams, L (2000) *Readymade Job Search Letters: All the letters you need for a successful job*, Kogan Page, London. This expert guide shows job-seekers how to write letters to land interviews. Aimed at the UK market. Also covers e-mail applications.

Yate, M J (2001) *Great Answers to Tough Interview Questions*, Kogan Page, London. Written by an ex search and selection consultant; as well as the executive briefing mentioned in this book, it is full of great tips on cover letters, CVs and interviews.

INTERNET RESOURCES

Online tests and tips

http://www.2h.com/iq-tests.html
Web site with links to IQ and personality tests. All tests are free and take from 12 to 20 minutes to complete.

http://mensa.org.uk
Web site for the Mensa high IQ society. You can register to take a local supervised test here and view extensive information on IQ tests.

http://testcafe.com
Contains IQ and EI tests. Short tests and brief results are free. Longer tests and detailed results reports start at about US $15.00.

http://emode.com
Web site dedicated to personality questionnaires for the purpose of improving domestic relationships. Some tests are free, though detailed results reports start at circa US $15.00. Good fun site.

http://queendom.com
Web site dedicated to personality and motivational questionnaires, IQ and EI tests. Some tests are free but full results reports and longer tests are charged by numbers of units. Applicants can buy units; prices start at circa US $2.95.

General and company search engines

http://www.google.co.uk
Free Internet search engine. Searches for company names, URLs and people's names.

http://www.msn.co.uk
Free Internet search engine. Searches for company names, URLs and people's names.

http://www.espotting.co.uk
Free Internet search engine. Searches for company names, URLs and people's names.

http://hoovers.com
Free company information site. Users can search by company name, industry sector, geography and turnover. A fee is charged for detailed or archived information.

http://search.yell.com/search/DoSearch
Free UK business search directory. Businesses can be searched for by sector, company name, location, or users can browse. Each search links to the company's URL if there is one.

http://www.companies-house.gov.uk
Government run companies' information site. Companies are searched for by name alone. Basic company information is free. This site has fantastic links to professional bodies such as the Association of Chartered Certified Accountants (ACCA).

http://www.tradepartners.gov.uk
Free government run site, part of British Trade International for helping UK firms attract overseas investment and encouraging foreign investment in UK companies. Companies can be searched for by A–Z of industries.

http://www.bestofbiz.com
London Business School run this business information service. Industry market data, latest business best practice news and executive briefings can be found here. Full company research is conducted for a fee.

Internet sources for industry-specific news

Accountancy

www.accountancy-uk.co.uk
UK focused accountancy news

www.accountancymag.co.uk
UK focused accountancy news

www.accountancyworld.com
International accountancy news

http://accountancy.workthing.com
Career focused news featuring interviews with accountants

Banking and finance

www.ft.com
UK focused latest financial news (*Financial Times*)

www.finance-uk.co.uk
UK focused financial news site

www.reuters.com/
US focused financial news

www.bba.org.uk
British Banking Association news site

http://banking.workthing.com
Career focused news featuring interviews with bankers

Catering

www.catering-uk.co.uk
UK focused catering news site

www.foodanddrinkeurope.com
European focused food and drink news site

www.caterer.com/news
UK focused catering news

Construction

www.construction-uk.co.uk
UK focused construction news site

www.engnetglobal.com/news
UK focused engineering site, covers civil engineering

Education

http://education.guardian.co.uk
UK focused education news (*Guardian*)

http://www.tes.co.uk
UK focused education news (*Times*)

www.canteach.gov.uk
UK teaching news and information site

http://education.workthing.com
UK focused teaching news

Engineering/manufacturing

www.newscientist.com
Engineering and scientific advancement news and information site

www.autoindustry.co.uk
UK focused auto industry news site

www.engnetglobal.com/news
UK focused news on various manufacturing engineering disciplines

www.foodproductiondaily.com
UK focused food production news site

www.engineering-uk.co.uk
UK focused engineering news site

http://engineering.workthing.com
Career focused engineering news, featuring interviews with engineers

Hotel and leisure sector

www.hospitalitynet.org
Hospitality news featuring market reports/financial and industry news

www.hotelinteractive.com
Internationally focused hotel news

IT

www.vnunet.com/
UK IT news

www.zdnet.co.uk/
UK IT news

www.silicon.com/
UK IT news

http://it.workthing.com
Career focused IT news featuring interviews with IT experts

Law

www.legal-uk.co.uk
UK focused legal news site

www.the-lawyer.co.uk
UK focused news for lawyers and solicitors

www.lawzone.co.uk
Latest news and legislation updates, UK focused

Marketing/media/advertising/publishing/PR

www.mad.co.uk/
Subscription based UK marketing news

www.marketingpower.com
Free marketing news site, sponsored by the American Marketing Association

www.theadstop.com
Free advertising news site, US based with an Internet focus

www.advertising-uk.co.uk
UK focused advertising news site

http://marketing.workthing.com
Career focused news featuring interviews with marketeers

PA/secretarial/admin

www.icsa.org.uk
For secretaries training in corporate governance/financial accounting
and law

http://admin.workthing.com
Career focused news featuring interviews with PAs and secretaries

Retail

www.simply-info.co.uk/
European focused retail and online shopping news

www.theretailbulletin.com
UK focused retail news

http://retail.workthing.com
http://sales.workthing.com
Career focused news featuring interviews with retailers and
sales experts

Telecoms

www.telcap.co.uk/
Free UK focused news

www.techWeb.com
Free US focused news

www.commstrade.com
Free UK focused communication technology news site

http://telecoms.workthing.com
Career focused news featuring interviews with telecoms experts

Travel

www.eyefortravel.com
Free e-travel news, UK focused

www.countryconnect.co.uk
Free international travel news

http://news.airwise.com
Free air travel news site

www.travelmole.com
UK focused online travel news

http://travel workthing.com
Career focused news featuring interviews with travel careerists

Generalist news-oriented Web sites

Business news

www.businessweekly.co.uk
UK focused business news

www.ft.com
UK focused business news (*Financial Times*)

www.telegraph.co.uk
UK focused business news (*Daily Telegraph*)

www.guardian.co.uk
UK focused news, particularly strong in government/non-profit, media and healthcare sectors (*Guardian*)

http://news.bbc.co.uk
UK focused news (BBC)

News focused on government and the non-profit sector

www.ukonline.gov.uk
UK government online news

www.fundraising.co.uk
UK focused fundraising news site

www.charitynet.org
UK focused news site for charities and government projects

http://government.workthing.com
UK focused government and non-profit news

Sites aimed at graduates

http://www.doctorjob.com
Graduates can search for internships or work experience jobs by degree subject area, location and industry sector.

http://www.workthing.com/info/graduate
Graduates can search for jobs by location, role, industry sector, company name and salary. There are lots of feature articles with various industry leaders on how they started their careers.

http://www.gradjobs.co.uk
This is the official Web site for Graduate Recruitment Fairs; graduates can search for fairs by location or sector. This site is a good source of information for graduates about companies that regularly recruit.

http://www.milkround.com
Graduates can search for jobs by sector, company name or location. Companies link to corporate sites or Graduate Recruitment Fairs if they are exhibiting, which facilitates company research for the user.

http://www.prospects.ac.uk
Graduates can search for job vacancies by role, location and company name. Company name searches link directly to vacancies and online application forms (if applicable). They can also search for internships, further study courses, and chat online to industry experts. They can also complete personality profile type questionnaires, which match them to suitable jobs.

Networking site

http://www.powermingle.com
Subscription to the Powermingle networking service is free. Users can profile their requirements under business or personal interests, and request contact from experts. Users can also check for industry events and conferences, and where appropriate enter a Mingle Zone for an event. If a user wants to search for and contact an expert, a subscription is charged at US $14.00 per annum.

CV tips sites

http://workthing-d-aspen.workthing.com/front/channel/changing_jobs/viewpoints/channel_front.xml
The 'at work' section of the Workthing site has up to the minute tips on CV writing, interview techniques and career management. Also features interviews with executives in all major sectors.

http://www.workthingcareers.com
Visit Working Careers' co-branded site for CV writing, interview coaching, career management services and advice. Working Careers provide a full range of PDFs to cover all aspects of career management; prices start at £4.95.

http://www.executivesonline.co.uk/candidates/cv.htm
This interim managers' job site has a fantastic example of an interim sales or marketing director's CV on it.

Appendix 2: Recruitment consultancies by industry sector and job seeker type

Sector	Agency name and URL	First jobbers/ graduate trainees	Second jobbers/ experienced hires/ executives	Senior managers/ executives/ experts/ board members
Accountancy, banking/ insurance & finance	Pertemps – www.pertemps.co.uk	X	X	
	Ellis Fairbank (all sectors) – www.ellisfairbank.com		X	X
	Joslin Rowe – www.joslinrowe.co.uk	X	X	
	Emerald Sky – www.emeraldsky.co.uk	X	X	
	Farlow & Warren Search & Selection – www.farlowandwarren.co.uk	X	X	
	Drax – www.draxexecutive.com			X

Table continued overleaf

Table continued

Sector	Agency name and URL	First jobbers/ graduate trainees	Second jobbers/ experienced hires/ executives	Senior managers/ executives/ experts/ board members
	Manpower (all sectors temp positions) – www.manpower.co.uk	X	X	
Catering/ food and drink manufacturing	Pertemps – www.pertemps.co.uk	X	X	
	Blue Arrow – www.bluearrow.co.uk	X	X	
Construction	Matchtech Group plc – www.matchtech.co.uk	X	X	
	Farlow & Warren Search & Selection – www.farlowandwarren. co.uk	X	X	
	Rullion – www.rullion.co.uk	X	X	
	Hill McGlynn recruitment – www.hillmcglynn.com	X	X	
Education	Pertemps – www.pertemps.co.uk	X	X	
	Select Education plc – www.selecteducation.co.uk	X	X	
Engineering and manufacturing	Pertemps – www.pertemps.co.uk	X	X	
	Matchtech Group plc – www.matchtech.co.uk	X	X	
	Connex Recruitment – www.connex-recruitment. com	X	X	
	Eldon Recruitment – www.eldonrecruitment. co.uk	X	X	
	XS CAD Recruitment – www.xscad.com	X	X	

	Rullion – www.rullion.co.uk	X	X	
	Drax – www.draxexecutive.com		X	X
Government, non-profit and public sector	Drax – www.draxexecutive.com			X
	People media – www.peoplemedia.co.uk	X	X	
Healthcare/ scientific	Recruitment Solutions Group – www.recruitmentsolutionsgroup.co.uk	X	X	
			X	X
	Ellis Fairbank – www.ellisfairbank.com	X	X	
	Key People – www.keypeople.co.uk			
	XS CAD Recruitment – www.xscad.com	X	X	
Hotel and leisure	Berkeley Scott Group – www.berkeley-scott.co.uk	X	X	
	Ellis Fairbank – www.ellisfairbank.com		X	X
	Quest Search & Selection – www.questsearch.co.uk	X	X	
IT	Matchtech Group plc – www.matchtech.co.uk	X	X	
	Connex Recruitment – www.connex-recruitment.com	X	X	
	Eldon Recruitment – www.eldonrecruitment.co.uk	X	X	
	Emerald Sky – www.emeraldsky.co.uk	X	X	
Law	Pertemps – www.pertemps.co.uk	X	X	
	Ellis Fairbank – www.ellisfairbank.com		X	X
	Joslin Rowe – www.joslinrowe.co.uk	X	X	

Table continued overleaf

Table continued

Sector	Agency name and URL	First jobbers/ graduate trainees	Second jobbers/ experienced hires/ executives	Senior managers/ executives/ experts/ board members
Marketing/ media/ entertainment/ advertising/ publishing and PR	Pertemps – www.pertemps.co.uk	X	X	
	Eldon Recruitment – www.eldonrecruitment. co.uk	X	X	
	Emerald Sky – www.emeraldsky.co.uk	X	X	
	Profiles Creative – www.profilescreative.com	X	X	
	New Media Careers – www.newmedia-careers. com	X	X	
	Drax – www.draxexecutive.com			X
PAs, secretaries and administrators	Pertemps – www.pertemps.co.uk	X	X	
	Ellis Fairbank – www.ellisfairbank.com		X	X
	FSS – www.fss.co.uk	X	X	
	Victoria Wall Associates – www.vwa.com	X	X	
Retail	Pertemps – www.pertemps.co.uk	X	X	
	Ellis Fairbank – www.ellisfairbank.com		X	X
	Retailmoves – www.retailmoves.com	X	X	
	STS Resource – www.stsresource.com	X	X	
Sales	Pertemps – www.pertemps.co.uk	X	X	
	Ellis Fairbank – www.ellisfairbank.com		X	X

	Eldon Recruitment – www.eldonrecruitment.co.uk	X	X	
	Emerald Sky – www.emeraldsky.co.uk	X	X	
Telecoms	Conexus – www.conexus.uk.com	X	X	
	Eldon Recruitment – www.eldonrecruitment.co.uk	X	X	
	Emerald Sky – www.emeraldsky.co.uk	X	X	
	Farlow & Warren Search & Selection – www.farlowandwarren.co.uk	X	X	
	Drax – www.draxexecutive.com			X
Travel and transport	Ellis Fairbank – www.ellisfairbank.com		X	X
	Matchtech Group plc – www.matchtech.co.uk	X	X	
	Emerald Sky – www.emeraldsky.co.uk	X	X	
	Quest Search & Selection – www.questsearch.co.uk	X	X	

Appendix 3

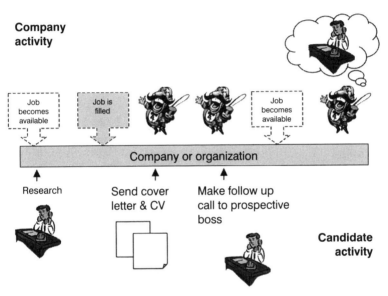

Appendix 3 *How to make speculative applications*

Index